Romania

A journey through a land of enchantment

By Howard D Richards

ISBN-13: 978-1518759932
ISBN-10: 1518759939

i

The book is about travels by car in 2011 through Romania with my wife, Cicely, and friends Roger and Linda Jackson.

I would to thank my friend Johanna Lockwood for proof reading the book.

Howard Richards
April 2016

CONTENTS

V

Romania

I knew very little about Romania except that in recent centuries the area was at the confluence of the Austro Hungarian Empire, the Russian Empire and the Ottoman Empire each one trying to gain territory from the other. In my studies I found out that it was a young country in its present state and was really a melange of different parts.

In 109 the region was a Roman province, Dacia, and consequently a large number of Latin peoples settled in it. The region retained its Latin roots to its language even though it was overrun in the third century by invaders from the east. Even so, the many peoples that infiltrated from the east, amongst them Goths, Huns, Bulgars, Avars and Slavs, have left distinct traces on both the land and its people. The core of the modern nation consists essentially of Wallachia and Moldavia and the former principality of Wallachia is shown as regions Oltenia and Muntenia on the map given on page 2. During the ninth century these two principalities formed the great Bulgarian kingdom, which in turn in 1019 became part of the Byzantine Empire that lasted until the invasion by Turks in 1456 when it was incorporated into the Ottoman Empire. The feudal nobility (boyars) in Wallachia retained the right to elect princes that lasted until 1726. In Moldavia though after the death of Stephan the Great in 1504 the former principality, which also included Bucovina, fell under the sovereignty of the Porte. Wars between the Ottoman Empire and Russia that started in 1768 and then continued on and off into the nineteenth century resulted in various exchanges of territory and domination until the Treaty of Berlin in 1878 when new borders were formally approved. In 1881 the Romania national government invited prince Carol of The Danube Principalities to be King of the new kingdom of Romania that consisted essentially of Wallachia, Moldova and Dobrogea.

Regions of Romania

The problem for Romania then lay with Transylvania for three million Romanian-speaking peoples were under the domination of the Austro-Hungarian Empire; moreover the Russians at the Treaty of Berlin took Bessarabia where a million others also lived. The history of Transylvania is even more complex and hard to understand, but I'll have a go to try to put it into context.

In the fourth and fifth centuries the Huns arrived in the Carpathian Basin from the Turanian Plain and established an Empire under their great leader Attila, whose bad reputation mainly derives from the Byzantine tales. As a result of these incursions the Székely people are one of the oldest cultures still present today in Romania. By the ninth and tenth centuries Hungarian royal authority was consolidated and the Székely were employed as frontier guardsmen. During the time of King Stephan's reign (the Saint sung about in the carol) the Saxons (Germans from the Rhineland) settled in the area. However, in 1241 the Mongols invaded and depopulated the country but even so the area began to flourish again under Hungarian rule. Vlach shepherds came over the mountains with their flocks of sheep and the Pope, Calixtus III, even described Hungary as the shield of Christianity. In 1526, Hungary fell to the Turks and Transylvania was spilt between Hungary and the Ottoman Empire. This state of affairs lasted until the end of the seventeenth century when the Turks were defeated outside the gates of Vienna. From that time onwards until the end of the First World War Transylvania became part of the Austro-Hungarian Empire. After WW1 reparations

Transylvania became part of Romania and this was ratified under the Treaty of Trianon in 1920. Hungary managed to get some of its previous land back in the inter-war years and by the end of WW2 Romania lost even more territory to the Axis powers as well as to the Soviet Union. Treaties at the end of WW2 returned northern Transylvania, lost in the inter war years, to Romania, but Northern Bucovina, Bessarabia and Southern Dobruja were not recovered from the Soviet Union. In 1947 the monarchy was abolished and a republic formed. Shortly afterwards Romania became a communist state that lasted until 1990 when the first democratic elections were held. Moreover in 1991 after the breakup of the Soviet Union its eastern and northern borders changed to independent republics of Moldova and Ukraine. However pro Russian feeling in the eastern part of Moldova across the Dniester River established a breakaway state of Transnistria that is not recognised by the UN and in 2014 pro Russian feeling in the Ukraine caused another breakaway state of Crimea to be established. Troubles in the Ukraine continue and likely further territorial losses may be incurred in the future. This illustrates the unstable situation in Romania's northern and eastern borders.

From this crude snapshot of history Romania can be viewed with wonder and curiosity. It has a whole lot of historical baggage including the recovery process from the aftermath of communist governance, as well as a considerable population of Roma People, even though half were eliminated in the Holocaust of WW2

The country is divided naturally by the Carpathian Mountains that form a crescent, as shown in the map on page 5. To the north and west of these mountains is the Transylvanian Basin that is generally over 1000 feet and undulating, the mountains rise to 8000 feet around it. To the south and east of these mountains is the riverine plain of the Danube and its tributaries. Further east is the Steppe of Dobrogea and in the far west the rich farm lands of Banat.

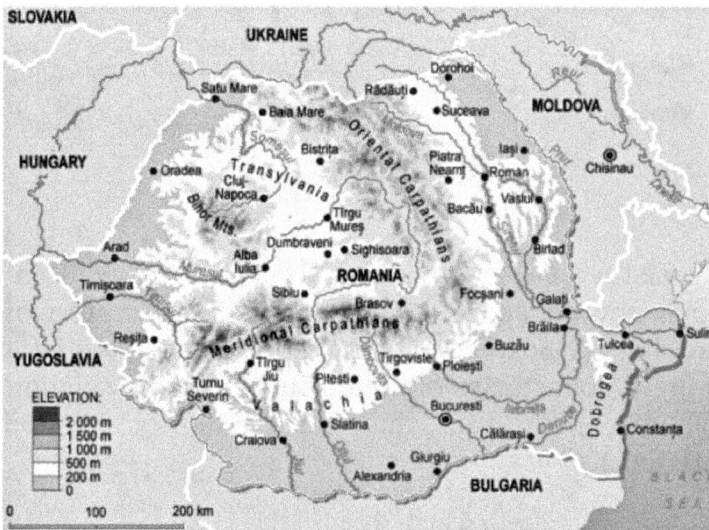

Topography of Romania

Route taken on travels

The history of Romania and its legacy, as well as its geography attracted us and our planned route would take in the Saxon Villages of Transylvania and the painted Monasteries of South Bucovina (the religion of Romania being in the vast majority Orthodox Christian).

Sinaia

It was early September 2011 and the sun was shining, as we drove north from Bucharest airport crossing a riverine plain following the E60, which was also designated Route 1. Our surroundings were dirty and neglected with many petro-chemical factories and oil wells with donkey pumps, a black pall of fumes hung in the sky. My mind drifted back to WW2, I remembered the raids on the Romanian oil fields taking place for Romania was the main supplier to Germany. It looked a horrendous place to live the noxious smell of the effluent was all pervading. Reaching the outskirts of the large industrial town of Ploiesti we by-passed it following a new dual carriageway to the west of the town. Thankfully, shortly afterwards we cleared the industrial mess around the town and emerged into farmland along the Prahova river valley heading towards distant mountains.

The Carpathians were covered in a blanket of in grey-white cloud and loomed larger as we headed north. Haymaking was taking place in open strip fields with men scything grass and herbage and in other strips ripe sunflower seeds were being harvested. There were fields of maize and even some vineyards. Trotting horses on the road pulled loaded carts behind them. They were made of wood, long and narrow and had pneumatic tyres fitted.

We were soon in the foothills climbing steadily when the dual carriageway gave out just before Comarnic. The valley narrowed and the mountains rose steeply above us. A short while later around seven in the early evening we arrived in Sinaia.

The New Montana Hotel is a large modern looking building with ample car parking space but had a flight of steps up to the reception area so not so good for carrying bags. Roger temporarily parked the car near to the steps for a hotel porter to take our bags up for us. By twenty to eight we had checked in and were walking down the Boulevard outside the hotel hoping to find a restaurant for the hotel had an event on and its restaurant was full. After turning up hill towards a Cable Car station saw nearby lights of a small restaurant that had both inside and outside tables, it was called 'Snow'. A waitress dressed in faux traditional costume showed us to a table, she was called Nicoletta and spoke good English. She took our order for 50cl glasses of Ursus beer, the local brew. It was good and turned out to be the first of a few while in Romania. Nicoletta left menus in English for us, although the translations weren't always understandable. Three of us chose grilled trout with lemon but Roger ever the meat eater chose to have pork kebabs instead that were served with onion. For a side dish I ordered frites this turned out to be a mistake for they were dry whereas the much better option would have been the 'peasant potatoes', which the girls shared between them; these are similar to a German potato salad except they are served hot with grilled bacon pieces added together with chopped dill, and taste delicious. Roger's kebabs were tough and not at all to his liking. There were one or two desserts to choose from but the crepes with citrusy soft green pistachio sauce went well with an espresso coffee. After saying our goodbyes to Nicoletta left for the hotel the air still warm but cloud covered the sky.

The next day I was up by six thirty after an almost sleepless night. I looked out to the street below and the steep wooded hillside opposite. Wispy white cloud drifted down the valley to the south and mist rose from the valley bottom. I put on the TV and watched the Telejournal of Romanian Channel One. There were pictures of people in ragged clothes looking none to happy. As far as I could fathom out the problem was contaminated rivers from old industrial plants and mines. The pictures skipped to another news story this time about poplar plantations being used for bio-fuel. Pictures again skipped this time to reconstruction of villages and towns; it was obvious that Romania was trying to improve the lot of its people.

Joining Roger and Linda for breakfast down on the ground floor near to reception Cicely and I were faced with a whole array of food to choose from. I selected pieces of melon, watermelon and pear for starters, as there was no cereal. Then I had some 'omletă', which was thick scrambled egg, and with it quarters of ripe beefy tomato and pieces of granary bread that I tried to

9

toast using a conveyor belt toaster, but only succeeded in warming the bread. The espresso coffee was served from a machine and was not as good as the night before. Roger being Roger sampled most of the hot items having egg, sausage and bacon and some cake too that he thought looked good.

Outside the sun was just breaking through the cloud, as three of us crossed the boulevard to the tourist office hoping to get information of what to do in the locality. No town maps were available and when we asked about the prospects of going up the mountain by the ski-lift a man behind the desk replied, *"It wasn't much use going up as the cloud wouldn't clear due to too much moisture in the air."* We left the office and walked up the street to a shop that sold maps that I had spotted the previous evening. The maps however proved to be no better than the one from the hotel. Cicely bought postcards and while she and Roger went back to the hotel I walked down the boulevard to find a post office. It was located in a side street and there a young attractive girl helped me buy the right stamps for postage to the UK.

After checking out of the hotel and packed all the bags into the car walked around to the cable car station to go up into the Bucegi Mountains. Across the road the Snow restaurant was open for breakfast. The price for tickets for the top and back was 62 Lei each with a two-stage journey. Sinaia's ski slopes are situated at an elevation of 2000m, the first cable car took us to the 1400m station where we stopped to take a brief look around before taking the second cable car to the top. The temperature had dropped considerably since leaving the valley bottom so put on our fleeces. Grey cloud limited the view, as we climbed a short rising grassy slope to look down into the western valley, as well as to the mountain panorama surrounding us. The ski slopes were obvious by their wear and lack of varieties of flora nevertheless we did see some dwarf azaleas and flowering gentians. Far below us a farm wagon trundled slowly along a mountain track heading towards the north. Shortly afterwards a flock of sheep moved steadily from the south attended by shepherds with white dogs. The sun appeared through some breaks in the cloud cover illuminating the mountainside in pools of light, but the cold air drove us back down the slope to the restaurant at the cable car station.

While sitting by observation windows drinking coffee saw more sheep gradually migrating across the lower slopes with two shepherds in attendance accompanied by large white mountain dogs. One of these sat on a knoll, sentinel like, watching the flock moving down into the valley beyond our view. Decorating the café-restaurant walls were old photographs of skiers and mountain walkers and judging from their clothing were taken in the 1930's era. Nearby on clothes hangers we spotted heavy natural sheepskin hooded coats draped on them, the thick natural wool side on the outside. Roger tried one on to our delight. It covered him completely transforming him to a good impression of a Yeti. This encouraged others in the café to try them on causing much hilarity, as they pranced around like bears in sheep's clothing.

It was one thirty when we took the cable car down the mountain, as the sun at last broke through the cloud cover. A young couple from Vancouver Canada who were in the car with us had been recently married, it was the girl's first trip back to Romania since she had left with her parents ten years before, when she was fourteen years old. They had been visiting a lot of relatives while on holiday and seemed extremely happy. In the morning they had visited Peleş Castle and recommended that we visit it too pointing it out to us set amongst pine trees far below and to the north west of the town above the valley.

Peleş Castle

Sinaia takes its name from the 17th-century monastery

built by a Romanian nobleman after undertaking a pilgrimage to Mount Sinai, Egypt. It was first mentioned in 1869 in documents, as a mountain resort. The beautiful region drew the attention of the Hohenzollern Royal House (Carol I - King of Romania) who commissioned Peleş Castle in 1873 for his summer residence. Prior to World War II and the abdication of the royal family, Sinaia became a summer retreat for most of Romania's aristocracy and many of their rather grand residences still remain as a sign of former glory days.

Reaching the bottom walked to the car and drove off to find the castle. Our inadequate map of the town was of no use and as a result got lost in the network of roads, as we headed up the mountainside. At a road junction I got out to ask a taxi driver who was parked up one of the roads. He directed me down hill again with instructions to take a left. The instructions appeared to be right for we came to an entrance gate beyond which was a large old building with cars parked outside of it. It was the Pelişor Castle Hotel, which is now part of the park complex to Peleş Castle. Roger paid a parking attendant some money that he seemed satisfied with.

A path took us through trees past a royal hunting lodge to the castle. My first impressions of the castle were of shock horror; it is an awful building that can't make up its mind what style it is. It is said to be German Renaissance mixed in with Italian Renaissance, Gothic, German Baroque, and French Rococo, and is an extreme example of architecture gone mad. The construction materials used were a mixture of wood, stone, brick and marble. Following tourist signs passed through the

13

main entrance into an inner courtyard. The ticket office was beneath an enormous lattice window, which had highly decorative carved wooden frames and supports, and on each side of the ticket office stood larger than life stone statues of very camp soldiers in pantaloons. Moreover, parts of the wall surrounds were also painted illustrating in part camp soldiers. We bought tickets for Option One that was a visit to the ground floor.

Standing under the gateway arch we waited for the door to open into the castle. Unfortunately when it did open a rather officious woman told us that the 'English Tour' would be another half an hour and only Romanians were allowed in. Having been given the brush off we looked around the grounds now illuminated by sunshine, the cloud now almost cleared away.

The Prahova Valley in which the castle stands is densely wooded. Beyond the stone balustrades, surrounding the terrace on three sides is a formal garden located in a clearing. It had a few roses and clipped hedges but at its centre was a statue of Carol 1 with hand on hip reflecting the camp style of the whole place. The third side of the terrace slopes steeply down to a park area. I walked along to the north side and descended some steps to a statue of Queen Elizabeta, Carol 1st's consort. She looked plump and rather stern, the artist portrayed her doing needlework, which she apparently was famous for. After looking at various shabby statues in the lower and upper terraces that were in need of a good clean and some very attentive maintenance work, if they are to survive more years I

14

went to find the others. I had passed Cicely earlier going down to the lower terrace area but Both Roger and Linda were near to the castle. We went together to the entrance door, as it was nearly time for our entry. Cicely arrived just in time when the officious woman came out to tell us that the English tour would be delayed again. I remonstrated with her and a little while later the door opened again and we were ushered in with other tourists.

In the reception area we were introduced to our male English-speaking guide. It turned out that he was good at his job and knew a lot of the detail yet wasn't forthcoming unless you questioned him, as he was on a timed tour. Our first piece of information was that the castle was the first building in Europe to have air-conditioning, electricity and ports for vacuuming, something for which they were very proud. The tour of the ground floor consisted of visits to ten rooms all of which had different influences in their design. We discovered that Elizabeta had considerable influence in the decor being an artist and poet of some fame. We saw rooms with Moroccan, Turkish, French, and Florentine influences, but much of it was too busy and over the top for my taste, nevertheless I could appreciate the Murano crystal chandeliers, the German stained glass, and the collection of Meissen and Sevres porcelain. But I wasn't so sure about some walls covered with Cordoba leather. There were ebony and ivory statues on display and carved wooden pieces plus a number of fine paintings, apparently the collection extends to 2000 pieces and is one of the finest in Europe.

Thanking our guide before we left we sadly abandoned the tour group who carried on their journey through the rest of the castle. The cloud had covered the sky once more as we left to find the car. Driving back down to the valley main road we noticed the proper entrance to the castle and noted if we had used it the walk to the castle would have been much further and up hill as well.

Moieciu Valley and Bran Castle

I estimated that Fundata would be an hour's drive away, however I hadn't counted on road works. Just north of Sinaia we met a traffic jam, nothing was moving and the time delay was considerable. It was a busy road for it was the main route to Braşov and into Transylvannia and road works in the small town of Buşteni had caused a considerable bottleneck.

Once clear headed north again through picturesque villages, the driving easy. On through Azuga and over the pass at Predeal at 1033m, Predeal being the highest town in Romania. Eventually we turned off the E60 to head west through the mountains on a recently resurfaced good road, the 73a, towards Râşnov. A number of hairpin bends had to be negotiated before we reached the north side of the mountains and by this time the sun was shining once more. Just outside of Râşnov was a junction with the E574, but it wasn't shown on our map, nevertheless we turned left heading in the right direction, southwest towards Piteşti. It was a glorious late afternoon, the high mountains before us once more.

Shortly afterwards we reached the village of Bran. The

castle there built in 1212 by the Teutonic Knights to guard the valley to the south that was used by traders. The castle loomed before us on a wooded hillside above the village where the road twisted through it. At the roadside were huts, stalls and cafés busy with traders catering for tourists. Passing through followed the road onwards towards the south going first along the Simon valley then the Moieciu valley, here and there charming villages with single storey houses decorated in different colours. Eventually we climbed steadily heading away from the valley along a ridge with fine views of both the Bucegi and Piatra Craiului mountains lit up in magnificent sunshine. From our search of the World Wide Web before departing the UK we established that there were a number of guesthouses in the area and from the information we had were looking for the Safir guesthouse in Fundata but after some trouble locating it saw a large notice stating it was for sale. Then turning back to what we thought of as the village centre spotted a four star guesthouse called Casa Muntelui.

Roger drove up a rough driveway and parked the car outside. It was a good-looking house built on three floors and looked as if it had ample number of bedrooms. A man came out, as Roger approached the entrance. He was middle-aged with a pot-belly and only had little English but nevertheless discovered that they had rooms. The man gave Roger a mobile phone so he could speak to someone in English. During the ensuing conversation he confirmed rooms for two nights and arranged for dinner. The en-suite rooms were situated on the first floor with the plentiful smart and clean furnishings including comfortable large size beds. After leaving our bags in the rooms went down to the dining room that overlooked the garden for an Ursus beer. A young man was outside holding a baby who seemed to be wide-awake. After finishing our drinks while the others went back to their rooms I had a good look around outside. Shortly afterwards a woman arrived whom I assumed was going to cook our evening meal.

Fundata is situated at the highest point of the pass, with an altitude, which varies between 1300–1400 meters. It's considered one of the highest settlements in Romania. I read somewhere that the main economical activity of the people living in Fundata from ancient times was and apparently still is, sheep and cow breeding, as well as milk processing. Nowadays though, tourism is a new and important activity that includes winter sports activities too, according to photographs and literature I had seen in the lobby. An interesting historical fact is that in WWI Fundata is where the first Romanian soldier died becoming the first war victim. At that time, Fundata was a border village between the Old Romanian Kingdom and the Austro-Hungarian Empire and allegedly some of the old border landmarks are still visible in the environs. In the communist period Fundata was one of the few places that did not experience 'collectivization' because it was considered that the land was not suited for 'model communist farms'. This meant that the people kept their land and their lifestyle. The place actually is best known for its cheese specialties for example the smoked cheeses and the Burduf that is wrapped in fir bark.

While walking around the property I breathed in the fresh mountain air and lapped up the last vestiges of sunshine. It looked a scattered community of farms and houses. Two houses opposite, across the narrow main road, had flowers in their gardens and both properties backed on to a hillside that was topped with fir trees. I could see sheep grazing in the field beyond one of the houses. Looking north and east from the garden towards the guesthouse were other wooded hills and between them a grassy col that probably led down into the Moieciu Valley. Close by a wooden barn had stacks of wooden planks outside and adjacent to it a farm with a collection of hayricks that had become the norm since we had been in Romania. Hay was stacked around fashioned wooden poles with a grass wreath on top and the grass surface combed to allow the rain to run off. It made them more compact than the English haystack and weather worthy too. But I would have loved to see them building them especially the taller ones.

After going back to our room for a shower and to change for dinner I went down into the small lounge adjacent to the dining room to read some of the books about the area. Linda and Roger arrived later and we were the only ones in the dining room but the young man was still outside in the garden with the baby obviously trying to get it to sleep but it was still wide awake and looking around. The woman I assumed to be the cook came to us and although she only had a few words of English managed to convey to us whether we would like some wine. A rack of wine was in the corner, we ordered a bottle of sauvignon blanc. Cicely was late coming down, as she had been unpacking the luggage. The wine was not cool enough nor was it dry but Cicely said it was OK for her. Roger got a merlot from the rack, which the woman opened for us smiling. Sitting down

20

to dinner at a quarter to eight four glasses of what I assumed to be Romania's version of raki were brought out to the table. It's slightly fiery and fruity made from some type of berry, possibly bilberry. The name for it is Pálinka and we were to get it in some form throughout the Transylvanian basin. It was lamb for dinner, this had been chosen earlier from a choice of lamb, chicken or pork.

The main course was pieces of grilled smoke flavoured mutton served with a pickled salad of cucumber and pepper together with some greasy chips. The flavour was good although the meat was tough, but the merlot went down well with. Roger was getting desperate he had struck unlucky for two nights running with pieces of meat stuck in his teeth. And Linda didn't like the pickled peppers. However, I liked it but I wouldn't say it was the best dish that I ever had.

Roger was on the mobile phone again brought out to him by the woman; he was speaking to the person that he had contacted before. It seemed that he was choosing the dessert and settled on some local dish. While we waited for it to be cooked our conversation developed to a discussion about colour. Roger, Linda and Cicely didn't agree with me when I said that the colour of the plastic water bottles was green. It seemed that the descriptions of colour are rather esoteric and subject to personal choice. Shades of green to blue are often difficult to describe. We didn't agree on the colour of the bottle but when the man came out he agreed with the others, so I was left colour blind according to them.

The delicious dessert arrived. The woman had cooked it from scratch. When we asked her what it was she wrote it down for me. It is a Transylvanian specialty called Papanaş. It was like a luscious donut with bilberry and served with cream. By now though we were on our second bottle of merlot and quite merry, still not agreeing on colour descriptions.

Papanaş

Ingredients:

400g sweet cottage cheese

4 spoons semolina

200-300g flour

2 tablespoons sugar

1 or 2 eggs

1 vanilla sugar (optional depending on different tastes) cooking oil cream and jam for serving

Process instructions:

- *Mix together the cottage cheese, semolina, 2 tablespoons of flour, the sugar and eggs (and the vanilla sugar as well, if you like the flavor)*

- *Then lay down a thin layer of flour on which you will put the crude "papanasi";*

- *Make small balls out of the mix and cover them in flour on the outside in order to prevent them from being sticky; put a hole in their center so in the end they should look like a torus (like a donut, if you like). Also make some smaller balls – these are to be placed on top of the donuts at the end. These balls should be a bit bigger than the hole in the donuts.*

- *Heat the oil, then fry the papanasi dough mix balls and the donuts you made. The oil should cover the content of the papanasi. You will see that the balls and "donuts" will rise – and when they do it's a sign they are done, but make sure to cook them on both sides.*

- *After baking every ball and donut, put on plates – each donut with a ball on top. Pour some cream on top and add jam on each "group". Voila! Ready to be served! As jam, you can choose wild cherry jam, fruits of the woods jam etc. – according to your preference.*

- *Preparing "papanasi" should take no more than 30 minutes mixing including baking. It is an easy desert to cook –and very tasty.*

  Some people avoid using semolina and use only flour. Others choose to grind the skin of half an orange to add to the mix, for an extra flavour.

We agreed to meet at eight for breakfast. Roger said that the girl had told him earlier that there would be cereal and eggs. We said our 'good-nights' but before going up to bed I asked the cook, who I began to think must be the owner of the place and possibly the girl on the phone her English speaking daughter, for extra pillows. She didn't understand this and brought me an extra duvet. I laughed and mimed a pillow she smiled and brought me two, I kissed her and went up to bed. It was quiet except for dogs occasionally barking, so had a good night's sleep in a very comfortable bed.

We were down for breakfast at eight where an arrangement of appetisers were placed on the table we had used last night. There was an array of slices of some dark coloured sausage, some battered cold meat, a dish of pork fat, slices of both tomato and cucumber and a basket of bread. The woman asked us what we wanted to drink when she brought in some myrtle jam and pieces of four types of cheese. Linda and Roger joined us and ordered their drinks too. There was no cereal but Roger requested to use the phone to speak to the girl. As a consequence of the call we ordered three omelettes, Cicely didn't want one. Coffee was brought out and a fruit tea for Cicely.

The breakfast was fine for me, the tomatoes fresh and tasty. I sampled before the omelette was brought out the cheeses, sausage and battered meat and one cube of pork fat that was difficult to digest. The coffee was good too.

After breakfast we left for Bran under a sky of thin wispy white cloud with the sun trying to break through. The weather forecast on TV said there would be sunny intervals with a temperature of 26 Celsius. A short while later after a drive along an empty road we arrived at the outskirts of Bran where we noticed a church being built, or restored, on the far side of the river. Roger parked the car alongside the wall to the castle grounds and from there we walked up into the village where stall keepers were already selling their wares, mostly tourist tat and cheeses. Carrying on around the walls we came to the castle's main entrance and followed a number of people up to the ticket office. Coach parties that we had seen evidence of on our arrival yesterday had fortunately yet to turn up. With our tickets we went on through the gate to the castle and walked up rough grey slate layered steps to a flat area on the castle hill that was surrounded by trees. The entrance to the castle was up a further flight of steps.

It is worthwhile recounting some of the history about the place, which is not associated with Dracula as portrayed by Bram Stoker, but it was obvious that this was a tourist money-spinner nevertheless. As I have already mentioned in 1212 the Teutonic Knights built the wooden castle of Dietrichstein, as a fortified position in the Burzenland at the entrance to a mountain valley through which traders had travelled for more than a millennium. I'll try to précis the information given in the entrance lobby.

"The Teutonic castle was destroyed in 1242 during the Mongol invasion. A document issued by Louis I of Hungary on November 19, 1377 appears to be the first written evidence of Bran Castle. It gave the Saxons of Kronstadt (Braşov) the privilege to build a stone citadel at their own expense and labour force; at the same time the settlement of Bran began to develop nearby. In 1438 -1442 the castle was used in defense against the Ottoman Empire, and later became a customs post on the mountain pass between Transylvania and Wallachia. It is believed Mircea the Elder of Wallachia briefly held the castle during which period the customs point was established. The Wallachian ruler Vlad Zepe

(Vlad the Impaler) 1448 -1476 does not seem to have had a significant role in the history of the fortress, although he passed by it several times through the Bran Gorge. Bran Castle belonged to the Magyar Kings but due to King Wladyslaw II's failure to repay loans the city of Brasov in 1533 gained strategic possession of the fortress, which remained important until the mid 18th Century. In 1920 the castle became a royal residence within the new Kingdom of Romania and was the favorite home and retreat of Queen Marie. In time the castle was inherited by her daughter, Princess Ileana, but was later seized after the expulsion of the royal family in 1948 by the communist regime. In 2005, the post communist Romanian government passed a special law allowing restitution claims on properties illegally expropriated, including Bran castle. In 2006, the government awarded ownership to HRH Dominic Archduke of Austria, Prince of Hungary, Prince of Tuscany, known commonly as Dominic Habsburg, the son and heir of Princess Ileana. He was an Industrial Designer then residing in New York State. However, in September 2007 an investigation committee of the Romanian Parliament stated that the retrocession of the castle to Archduke Dominic was illegal, for it broke Romanian law on property and succession. The decision changed yet again in October 2007 when the Constitutional Court of Romania rejected parliament's petition on the matter that led in turn in December 2007 to the Romanian government issuing a U-turn decision reaffirming the validity and legality of the restitution procedures used and confirming that the restitution was made in full compliance with the law. On May 18 2009 Bran Castle administration was transferred from the government to the administration of Archduke Dominic and his sisters Maria-Magdalena Holzhausen and Elisabet Sandhofer. On June 1st the Habsburg's opened the refurbished castle to the public as the first private museum in the country and announced with Bran Village's local government a joint strategic venture to ensure that Bran was on the growing tourist circuit, thus assisting the economic base in the region."

So the ex Royal Family of Austro-Hungary was generous to the people of Romania. We didn't go on a guided tour but found our own way around the various rooms and floors occasionally listening in on tour guides but there was also information in English on the main display boards. The rooms had simple furnishings, information about genealogy, old photographs when it was a royal residence, old clothing from the royal period in glass cabinets, tiled heaters and windows looking out on to the surrounding countryside. The second floor accessed by a very narrow staircase had a loggia surrounding three sides of an inner courtyard. I met Roger on the way down to the inner courtyard but he stayed on the first floor waiting for the girls who were somewhere on the top floor. I sat on the wall surrounding the well. Several Romanians came up and threw money down into it, mostly coins but notes too probably only a few lei at most. Then a group of English people arrived. I discovered that they were railway enthusiasts and were on holiday from Yorkshire to explore some of the Romanian steam trains and lines. Their visit to Bran was just a diversion for them. Currently they were staying at Braşov. I wished them well and walked over to look around the small shop while waiting, but as soon as the others joined me we all walked back down the steps to the village to look around the market stalls and shops. The castle wasn't at all what I had expected, the furnishings minimal, the profile with the towers not quite like the horror movie portrayals of Count Dracula, perhaps though on a dark thundery night one's imagination could run riot. I wasn't disappointed for some of the features I liked very much such as the loggia surrounding the small inner courtyard.

One of the shops was making and selling spiral type cakes that a fiend, Joy Bishop, told us to look our for. These are called kürtöskalács.

Kürtöskalács

The worldwide famous Kürtöskalács is a traditional Hungarian pastry originating in Transylvania. I have encountered a very funny renaming of the Kürtöskalács, on the web: the "Barbecued Chimney Cake". Kürt is Hungarian for horn and kalács means milk bread. These tasty Transylvanian treats are giant rolls made of dough covered with caramelized sugar and walnut, coconut and many other toppings. Kürtöskalács is made in smaller rolls too, so people can taste more flavors. It is sold in specialized stands, at street corners, in open markets and occasional fairs, or you can make it yourself.

Ingredients:

1000g flour

500 ml lukewarm milk

50 g yeast

6 egg yolks

100-120 g butter

1/2 tbsp. salt

2 tbsp. sugar

crushed nuts, coconut, almonds

Process Instructions:

Step 1: Dissolve the yeast in the lukewarm milk and let it rise.

Step 2: Beat the egg yolks and melted butter together, and add the salt and sugar.

Step 3: Add the egg mixture and the yeast to the flour and blend together thoroughly.

Step 4: Cover with a cloth and leave it in a warm place to rise.

Step 5: When done, roll it out and cut into 3 cm wide, long strips.

Step 6: Wrap the strips one by one around a cylindrical mold brushed with oil.

Step 7: Push and roll this spiral to press the strips so that the edges

29

nearly meet.

Step 8: Brush these spirals with oil or melted butter and roll in sugar.

Step 9: Bake over open coals (if possible), or in an infrared oven.

Turn the spirals constantly so that each part gets evenly browned. When they are perfectly caramelized, they are taken off the coals and rolled in crushed nuts, cinnamon, coconut or simply, in more sugar. This last additional topping is not really necessary for they taste great with just the plain caramelized sugar glaze.

We stopped to look at a woman making them and Roger bought one for us to sample; it was placed in a brown paper bag for us. Over the road we found a café-bar and ordered coca cola and a peach fruit drink for me. Roger gave us pieces of the kürtöskalács to eat with our drinks. It tasted good, crispy, and spicy with coconut and some other nut flavouring, from the sugary sprinkling on the surface of the spiral.

We didn't finish the entire bread spiral so Roger carried the paper bag with the remains. A small dog with short legs and a long bushy tail, typical of the dogs we had seen around in the village, probably feral, drawn by the scent followed Roger happily, almost with a smile on its face looking up at the paper bag expectantly, as we walked back through the village passing where we had parked the car to go across the road to an open park area in the valley. Roger didn't give in to the dog's quiet pleading and tail wagging for he wanted some more himself. The dog eventually gave up after we had crossed the road to cross a footbridge over the river to a freshly mown grassy area, possibly used for football by village youngsters. On the other side of it was a raised platform positioned beneath a hill, it looked like a bandstand. From there we got a good view of the castle. Walking southwards further down the valley we passed some ruins and a small domed church to an area where there were two long huts looking like leftovers from military use. One of these looked better cared for than the other. The less cared for one was dilapidated and from the outside looked as if it was near to giving up the ghost, it was indeed a hovel. An old crone, probably a Gypsy, came out and put some washing on a strung out line then began cutting wood for a fire outside. Our interest lay though in the church a little further down the valley.

The roof of a multi-domed and turreted church was under construction; three men were on the roof and one on the ground directing the action. The outer walls had only their cladding to be completed. Both Cicely and Linda thought the action of the men on the roof a little precarious. They were fitting a large beam as part of the roof support in situ. One man held the beam in place while the other used a chain saw above him to trim it to size. While we looked on, the roof-beams for one turret were completed. On the other side of the river we spotted some sculptures and crossed over to see them close up. They were placed in a narrow strip of grassland between the river and the tree-lined road. The materials used were wood and iron, the latter now rusty brown in colour. The sculptures included a more than life size statue of a standing man with his arms hanging down and palms forward, a horizontal wooden statue I think of Christ nailed to vertical wooden posts, and a large wooden hand. I can't remember how many others there were but five six I think.

31

Leaving Bran we headed north towards Raşnov along route 73 heading out of the mountains across flatter country. Behind Raşnov on a wooded hill stood a castle. The citadel built according to our guidebook around the year 1215 (the date of the signing of the Magna Carta in England) by the Teutonic Knights and it is mentioned in known papers for the first time in 1331. The citadel was conquered only once in its history, around the year 1600 by Gabriel Báthory. However, when we got closer to the town we saw Raşnov painted in large white letters on a sign beneath the castle spoiling the whole effect.

Road maintenance work was being carried out causing delays. One lane of the road surface was being tarmacked. Some of the drives to the town houses were also being done but mostly they looked as if they would be left with a ramp down to a stony surface. It was a small town and we were soon through it heading towards Braşov fifteen kilometers away. At the side of the road some men and women both young and old were selling berries in pots.

Cicely and I had seen an awful video clip about the city before leaving home. It was produced by a man who obviously hated it and warned people away saying it had high unemployment, a lot of crime and a lot of graffiti and was an entirely unloved place, dark and dismal. I wasn't looking forward to going there from the impression the video clip had given.

Following signs to the City Center we eventually arrived in the central part of the old town tucked under Mount Tampa on the edge of the pedestrianized Piata Statului. It was difficult finding a place to park the car but eventually managed to park at the edge of a road just past Parcul Gheoghe Dima. From there we walked directly back to the pedestrianized square and called in at the information tourist office situated in Casa Statului, just off the square. Glancing at the town map we were given we agreed on a visit to the Black Church, an ancient gothic cathedral that was close by.

The Black Church, Marienkirche, has had a turbulent history. It was built between 1385 and 1477 on the site of a much earlier church that was destroyed during Mongol invasions in 1242 and its reconstruction was hampered by the extensive damage caused by Turkish raids in 1421. According to our guidebook the church was given its new name after disaster struck yet again in 1689, when a 'Great Fire', set by Hapsburg (Austro-Hungary) invaders, leveled most of the town. The church was damaged, blackening its walls and its restoration took almost 100 years.

The church was surrounded by an area of loose stony gravel and looked the worse for wear with many of its former statues missing. Inside a display of carpets looked incongruous but allegedly it is the richest collection of Anatolian carpets in all of Europe dating from the 17th and 18th centuries. They were produced in the famous carpet weaving areas of Brussa, Uschak and Ghiordes and donated to the church by merchants travelling in the Orient. Although the carpets were interesting, they couldn't be viewed close up, and in spite of its claim to be the tallest Gothic church between Vienna and Istanbul I didn't like it.

All of us, I think, a little disappointed with the church

visit and walked back up the road towards the car. Near to Parcul Gheoghe Dima a wrought iron gate led into a seating area of a café that was enclosed by iron railings Entering bought ice creams, I had a scoop of vanilla and one of dark chocolate served in a plastic tub. It was pleasant to sit in the shade provided by trees eating ice cream but I didn't like what we had seen of Braşov. Had we done it justice? I doubt very much for the surroundings of wooded hills do give it a better feel.

We left Braşov following signs indicating Piteşti then on through Raşnov where tarmacking was still in progress and on towards the mountains where white cloud gathered on some of the summits but generally it was fine and warm, a glorious sunny afternoon. Through Bran, still busy with tourists, and on past the church, where the men were still working on the roof, towards Moieciu passing by colourful one storey houses in the village to turn off to our left keeping to the valley heading for Moieciu de Sus. The valley is beautiful penned in by green hillsides topped with woodland. The number of pensions and guesthouses was overwhelming though and seemed too many to be economically viable. They were decked with flowers and the gardens of the houses grew many too of all shades and colour. In the village parked by a church that was situated within a walled enclosure and walked through a gateway set into the roadside wall to view it close up. The church wasn't open but outside its walls displayed a fresco frieze of religious and farming scenes. These colourful illustrations made the small country church with its little spire delightfully romantic moreover the grounds surrounding it were like a

34

flower garden in full bloom with gravestones set within. One particular monument to death erected against one of the surrounding walls was constructed in marble and dedicated to someone who died young, just before her forty-fifth birthday. It was both stunning and moving.

Continuing our drive up the valley climbed steadily through an attractive rural landscape of green hills with wooden fences separating fields perpendicular to the contours of the steep hillsides below which red-topped three storey houses gleamed in the sunlight. Driving on past a road that led to Fundata holiday complex we took a left fork where the river valley became wooded and more enclosed. A red fox cub sat in the road scratching its fur undeterred by our arrival; further on the road petered out. Returning to the fork in the road we explored where the other road took us before going back to the turn off to the holiday complex. In Roger's mind was the possibility that there might be a way over the hill to where we were staying so it would be good to explore to see if this was feasible.

The tarmac road gave out after 100m and we continued along a wide stony track climbing and winding our way though dense woods up the mountainside for about 5km until we reached the complex of Cheile Gradistei. It is located on a plateau near the top of the mountain where we were greeted by a number of notices that indicated different locations including hotel, sauna, gym pub, games area, and restaurant. It looked a good spot for a winter holiday, or for mountain walking. A number of groups of people wandered around but we continued driving to the top to park in a large area at the bottom of some steps that led up to a restaurant. The panoramic view to the south and east was quite spectacular, mountain crags shining white in the late afternoon sunshine. Inside, the restaurant had a huge dining room with many people at tables eating and drinking. At the bar ordered large glasses of a local dark beer to sit and drink at one of the tables. Peering around us saw food being served in large quantities, probably for mountain walkers who needed it.

After further explorations of the site soon found out that there was no drivable way down to Fundata and possibly the only way down was by a steeply descending path designed for walkers. So it was back down the stony road for us but in a much shorter time than our ascent. Arriving back in Moieciu de Sus we admired one of the pensions built in chalet style with five storeys. It had window boxes of flowers on every floor and what made it more remarkable were large frescos on both sides of the building depicting village life, celebrating food from rearing to eating and illustrating people in traditional dress.

Back on Route 73 headed for Fundata but stopped beneath an area of land above the road on which a small wooden church was located. Masses of wild flowers still in bloom surrounded it. Our access was by some wooden houses bordered by a wooden fence. These enchanting houses had dormer-windows set into wooden shingle roofs. A sign in a garden stated 'Slow Food' and a young woman came out to look at us querying whether we wanted something I replied were just going to look at the church. In retrospect it would have been good to make a visit to see the insides of the houses.

Wooden Church

A path led to the church through an ornate carved wooden gateway with wooden roof. The architecture was fascinating. The church although small displays enormous power. It's built on a wooden platform with plank walls and at the entrance end, facing south, is a little terrace with four wooden pillars each pair having railings between them and between the center a gap with three steps for access. The roof overhung the sides and a second roof is stacked on top of it, moreover surmounting the top roof is a square cross-sectional tower open at the top but fitted with a pyramidal roof that overhung it. The whole effect was quite pleasing. Unfortunately, the church was not open to see the inside but the outside dramatic, especially since dark clouds covered the sky with still a little sunshine braking through at a low angle, for it was early evening. The grounds weren't extensive but within them a wooden square cross-sectioned structure with a roof supported by four pillars housed a wooden representation of Christ on the Cross.

Arriving back at Casa Muntelui discovered dinner would be served at seven thirty so there was just time for a quick shower and change of clothing. I was the first down and started writing my diary. Linda was the next to arrive with Roger fast on her heels. I went to fetch Cicely for the dinner of chicken with gravy and polenta was being served. Got another bottle of merlot from the rack but we couldn't make the woman understand about the unfinished bottle of white from last night, so ordered as well small carafe of white for Cicely. The chicken didn't satisfy our hunger so it was a phone call again to the girl who spoke English. Roger indicated that we wanted some cheese and bread besides the crepes for dessert. Four types of cheese were brought out with some segments of tomato, pickled cucumber and pickled pepper and plenty of bread. This satisfied our hunger and allowed the wine to be finished with some vigor for the missing bottle of white was brought out too. The crepes when they arrived were good too served with a fruit jam. It turned out that Roger also reminded the girl that we wanted cereal and fruit for breakfast in the morning.

On the way up to bed met the young couple who were obviously staying there and who had the active baby. It was still awake and we had a laugh about it, but I was glad that our days of walking babies were over. The

38

man was going down stairs again with the baby trying to get it to sleep.

The next day we were all down for breakfast by eight. The table had been laid and had cornflakes and muesli on it plus a very large bowl of green grapes and red plums. Madame was all smiles and seemed pleased when she saw us looking appreciatively at it all. When Linda and Roger arrived she served coated deep fried cheese, sausage, and the various salads and some bread. The sky had cleared a little when we settled our bill that Madame hand wrote. The bill for two nights accommodation, breakfast and dinner was only 240 Lei per room per couple and a total of equivalent of £100 for all the food and wine and beer consumed over the two days, an absolute bargain.

Cisnãdioara and Sibiu

It was Friday driving north at first to the outskirts of Raşnov noting how well the workmen were getting on at the church in Bran. From Raşnov headed northwest down the 73A bypassing Zarneşti and carrying on along a rough road through a wooded secluded valley. Dense forests hereabouts are reputed to have lynx, bear and wolves in them. There were some small farms with tiny fields. People were mowing with scythes with some stacks of hay already built. The villages passed were long and linear with single storey houses rendered in different shades of ochre. When we reached Şinca Nouã, a picturesque village, it was a hive of activity with horse drawn carts supporting the local agrarian economy. We turned towards Şeraia, the road straight on led to Victoria where there is a notorious chemical plant built in communist times. I was glad we weren't going anywhere near it, but discovered later from the owner of the place we were to stay that the chemical plant is now closed down and as a consequence has caused large unemployment in the area around Fãgãraş.

We hadn't been able to refuel the car as many fuel stations along the road were out of fuel and had to drive on to Făgăraş amongst truck traffic to find a service station that had some for sale. A large golden dome dominated the skyline as we approached the town along Highway 1 and found it was a church in the town centre.

There is a fascinating description of how the town got its name. 'The name is alleged to derive from the Romanian word for "beech", (fag). Another explanation of the name is alleged to derive from the Hungarian language word for "partridge", (fogor). But a more plausible explanation is that the name is given by Fogaras River coming from the Pecheneg, "Fagar šu", which means ash water. Yet another source of the name is given by folk etymology to be Hungarian, as the rendering of "wood" (fa) and "money" (garas), with legends stating that money made of wood had been used to pay the peasants who built the fortress around 1310.

Its history is interesting too, as is the state of the town today. Făgăraş during the Middle-Ages, together with Amlaş was an established Romanian enclave in Transylvania but after the Tatar invasion in 1241-1242 Saxons settled the area. In 1369, Louis I of Hungary gave the Royal Estates of Făgăraş to his vassal Vladislav I of Wallachia and the territory remained in the possession of Wallachian Princes until 1464. During the rule of the Transylvanian Prince Gabriel Bethlen (1613-1629), the city became important in the southern regions of his realm and Făgăraş became the residence of the wives of Transylvanian Princes. An equivalent is Veszprém, the Hungarian "City of Queens". At the beginning of the 20th century the town was ethnically mixed with 3357 Hungarian, 2174 Romanian and 1003 German peoples living there. Later the Communist State used Făgăraş's castle as a stronghold, but during the 1950s it was converted to a prison for political opponents and dissidents before being converted to a museum in recent times. After the fall of the Communist State in 1989 the city's economy was badly affected by the closure of most of its industries and is now one of the poorest municipalities in Romania.

Arriving in the town we parked outside of a café-bar near to the church. The church had considerable scaffolding erected around it suggesting it was being restored. Sitting at a table inside ordered drinks. After I finished mine I went over to a large building that was supposed to house a tourist information office, but found it closed. The whole place looked run down. I crossed the busy road again and headed for the money exchange and changed some English Pounds for Lei at a good rate of 4.7. It was gloomy in the town so we didn't stop to look around any further and carried on our way westwards.

The sun was now shining through large patches of blue sky and had intended to have lunch at Sibiu before going on to find accommodation, but the time was creeping onwards. Stuck behind slow moving traffic with no easy place to overtake Roger was in need of a lunch break and a rest. The countryside was open and hilly with mountains to our left and to our right in the distance flowed the large River Olt, which we could see at times especially when there were lakes. The mountains, part of the Carpathian Chain, were locally known as the Făgăraş Mountains. Ahead of us ranged other hills that were the Muntii Cindrei with elevations over 2000m. We passed large fields of maize, dried sunflowers, and potatoes that were being hand picked and placed in sacks before loading onto carts. Quite a few workers were in the fields gathering the crop. When we reached the north south road, route 7, between Sibiu and Drăgăşani that passed through the mountains in one of the few good passes we turned northwards heading towards Sibiu. After a few hundred meters turned into the car park of a transport restaurant.

A large family party of eight had arrived just before us and it took us a long time to be served, but we managed to get drinks while we looked at the menu. Fortunately it had an English translation. Both Cicely and I wanted omelets but they were now off the menu so Cicely decided she didn't want anything else, but I ordered sausage with farmhouse potatoes. Linda ordered some traditional dish with egg, meat and polenta and Roger ordered beans and ham. The usual tomato and cucumber salad was also served with meals. I gave mine to Cicely only for Roger to give me his, as he doesn't go much on the salad stuff. Cicely had some of Linda's food too but in the end the quantity of food was just too much.

After lunch we drove a little way on towards Sibiu before turning west along a country road to Cisnădie that climbed steadily into the hills. The girls had the print out for the guesthouse we were looking for, but not realizing that it was in the Commune of Cisnădie and not the village itself. We drove around the village but found no signs to it, so Roger parked the car in the central square. I walked into a shop that also indicated 'Tourist Information'. They quickly spotted our mistake for the guesthouse was located in Cisnãdioara not Cisnãdie. Driving further into the hills spotted a few pensions on the way, but not the one we were looking for. Eventually we arrived in the village centre with an open area of rough stone. There was no signs for the guesthouse we were looking for but there was one a to a 4-Star guesthouse that Linda suggested we look at. Roger turned down a bumpy track that led us after a short distance to Casa Belevedere.

Casa Belevedere from the outside was a three-storey house black and white timber framed with green shutters, which we discovered later over dinner, was not old but of recent build. An upward sloping driveway ran along its long side where a covered walkway above the drive allowed access to rooms. Nobody was around so I continued on upwards to another building that had 'Reception' posted on it. Inside a large number of people gathered around a long refectory table having lunch. It was sometime before they gathered I was a tourist looking for rooms. Fortunately one of the men in the party spoke a little English and said he would go and find someone to help me.

A short while later an attractive middle-aged woman came up from the lower building to greet me. Her name was Stella and spoke only a little English but had some French too. She said to follow her and we left to climb steps up to the inner covered walkway I had seen earlier to take me to see the rooms. The rooms looked good and well appointed with en-suite facilities. I then asked her about a restaurant. She replied that they served dinner and that the breakfast was a buffet. That evening dinner would be soup plus fish with lemon and potatoes. The rooms were available for three nights, so I said that I would go and fetch the girls to look at the rooms explaining to her that we were parked outside by the church.

Back at the car I explained the situation to all and both Linda and Cicely returned with me to see the rooms. But on meeting Stella once more she first took us through the 'Reception' area, where people were still eating, to the other side into a small courtyard and up some steps to a large outdoor swimming pool that was solar heated. Beyond the pool a path led up to a garden area with children's swings and barbeque facilities. Having shown us the extensive grounds and facilities Stella took us to see the rooms in the main house.

The girls were impressed with the rooms and by this time Roger had arrived on the scene. He thought the price was a little steep but Stella explained about all the facilities again. It wasn't difficult to persuade Roger to agree to take the rooms and we agreed with Stella to have dinner at seven-thirty and breakfast at eight.

Roger having driven up the driveway to make it easier for us we unloaded the bags into our respective rooms. He was told that he could park up near reception but preferred to leave the car outside by the church. After a short break set off again to explore the surrounding area. Whilst talking with Stella had noticed that a small group, a young woman with several kids in tow, was selling buckets full of blackberries, Stella bought some. It was only later after dinner that we discovered that they were Roma and that they lived in their own village in the woods that was located further up the track from Cisnădioara from which they had been expelled many years ago. Roger drove around the village and up the track where the blackberry gatherers had disappeared. The track soon deteriorated and brought us to a halt.

Something was happening in the field and stream below us. Men were working there cutting wood but a horse hitched to a cart had ideas about a drink, or eating the green grass on the far side of the stream and took off towing the cart down a steep slope to the streambed where it stopped. A little later one of the men in the field went over to it unhitched the horse from its tangled state and sorted out the cart. It seemed no time at all before the horse and cart were trundling up the track to where the horse and cart had been originally parked. This was a little snapshot of country life that we were to experience throughout our period in Transylvania.

Roger drove out of the village heading for Sibiu, the local large town. While passing through the village we looked out for the restaurant listed in the 'Lonely Planet' guide, Hanul Pinul. Its location was supposed to be on the Sibiu road and according to the guide it had fine views of the countryside and of the Citadel in Cisnădioara, which are said to be especially fine at nighttime when the Citadel is floodlit. We never did find the restaurant, but we did see signs to another, Apfel House B&B and restaurant up a narrow track road off the 106D road.

A rural road took us through wooded countryside and up and over a hill to a main road where we turned towards Sibiu heading again through woods that according to the map were part of the 'Parcul Natural Dumbrava Sibiului'. At the outskirts to the town the road changed into a tree-lined boulevard that took us eventually to Piaţa Unirii, a convenient large car park nearby.

Pedestrianized Street in Sibiu

A pedestrianized street led to the town's historic centre passing by shops and cafes to a large square called Piaţa Mare, which had intermittent gushing fun fountains within it. The town was clean and well cared for and had a number of fine buildings. I had read that the city had been restored to some glory a few years previously when it was a 'City of Culture' for a year, as part of Europe's City rounds. Compared with Brasov it looked in an entirely different league. Crossing the

48

square to the Tourist Information Centre I asked about maps. They didn't have any but told me about which Saxon villages to see and a little about the Transfăgărașan Road. A young man there also told us that the speed of cars using the famous road averaged only 5mph so that it was only practical to do the north side of the mountain range, which he thought was the most attractive anyway. He directed Roger and myself to the Libaria Schiler, a university bookshop across the square where we would find suitable maps for sale. A little while later while the girls took photos in the square Roger and I were browsing the shelves in the bookshop. Eventually I found a good map of the Saxon Villages and bought it.

Outside the sky was darkening to pewter and threatening rain with a strong cool wind blowing off the mountains, but there were one or two clear blue patches of sky still with the sun shining dramatically through them illuminating the street and architectural features of the buildings. About half way down the pedestrianized street, towards Piața Mare found an attractive café-bar to sit drinking outside watching people as they passed by, most of them young people, possibly students from the local university.

Not long afterwards on the road again driving back to Cisnădioara. The sky had cleared resulting in a fine sunny warm evening. It didn't take long to get back to the guesthouse and agreed to meet for drinks in the dining room at seven fifteen so had time to properly unpack and have a leisurely shower.

By the time we all arrived in the dining room at the end of the building near to reception it was time for dinner.

It was a large dining room with one couple already eating there. A young woman introduced herself to us. She was Stella's niece, called Nadina, and showed us to a long table. She spoke good English and we soon discovered that she was studying law, having already attained her Bachelor Degree, and was now working in a solicitor's office in Sibiu during the continuation of her studies. She was about 22 and wore tight black leggings that showed off her trim svelte figure, but a short blouse top gave her the look of some medieval waitress. Whilst chatting about the locale and what we hoped to do from the visit to Romania she served us two carafes of local wine one white and one red produced by a Frenchman from Bordeaux, who has a vineyard and winery in Transylvania. The wine we found drinkable and quite pleasant especially with the various dishes of food that were then brought out.

Soup was served first in a large tureen. It was tomato and carrot based with meatballs. Side dishes of chili peppers, sour cream and bread were served with it. Next came a main course of deep fried battered perch served with capers, half lemons and boiled potatoes with a side salad each of sliced tomatoes, sliced cucumber and peppers. Both the first and main courses I found very good and satisfying. The dessert consisted of six soft biscuits with jam centres and chocolate bases.

While finishing off the wine, the red carafe having been replenished, over coffee, Stella's husband, Peter, dropped in for a chat. We soon discovered that he was from a Saxon background and that German was his second language but he also spoke French and

Hungarian too. His English was better than his French so we conversed easily. The conversation stretched over many interesting and fascinating topics with him telling us about the region, the best villages to see, but he also put us off visiting the Roman town ruins that I had planned by saying that they weren't worthwhile. During the time spent with him we discovered that most of the education in the region was provided by German schools but also found out that the Hungarian peoples didn't go to these preferring instead Romanian schools. He told us a little of the history of the area since the Roman occupation and the current ethnic mix of peoples including the Roma people and said we should visit Brateiu on our journey through the Saxon villages to see their copper work and marked its location on our map with his other suggestions. Raising the topic of religion I discovered that it wasn't stamped out under communist rule only hidden from view and now many churches were being restored. He told us about corrupt politicians, where projects required three times the cost to satisfy various bribes and pay-offs. Mentioning what we had seen in the Moieciu Valley by way of the number of 'Pensiuneas' he informed us that there were indeed too many in the current economic climes and that some were closing down and that the construction industry had been severely affected. We agreed to stay for dinner the next day for it would be barbequed pork.

We had had a full day with many ideas formulated over dinner for the next day, which was going to be hot and sunny. Nadina, the cook and Stella in the darkness within the enclosed walkway to our rooms were smoking cigarettes. We said goodnight as we passed looking out onto a brilliant starry night to go to bed.

Saxon Villages

The next day at the Casa Belevedere I woke to a clear pale blue forget-me-not sky, a lovely morning and the village still and peaceful. At the buffet breakfast Nadina came in dressed in her black tights smiling and asking us whether we would like coffee or tea. Cicely had written some postcards to send home to friends and relations and asked where to post them but Nadina said she would take care of it but they wouldn't go until Monday (later we discovered that one of these cards took over a month to arrive at its destination in the UK) saying that the post was usually good and that I had put the right stamps on them. Roger also asked about washing his trousers and Nadina said she would take care of that too. After breakfast we set off on a tour of the Saxon Villages.

It was a fine and glorious day as we drove towards Sibiu taking the same route as yesterday. Arriving at the town we took the D14 that skirted the old town to head northwards through countryside of wooded rolling hills and grassland sharing the road with horses and carts. Some of the hills had overgrown terraces suggesting a much different agricultural usage in the past. Flowering yellow golden rod and rudbekia like flowers covered the banks of streams and smothered some of the hillsides too.

Our first stop was the village of Slimnic and on a signpost to the village its German name of Stolzenburg was also given. A brown sign indicated the fortified church to our right up a stony track. On a hill, they call Burgbäsch, we could see a stone tower with a red tiled pyramidal roof set within ruined high stonewalls that surrounded the place, there was also a hint of other ruins. Roger drove up the track to park near to the historic remains where paths led up through a dried parched looking grassy hillside. Our individual explorations took different routes around the walls. I climbed the sunny side making for the base of the walls from which I had good views of the village below. Wild plants were flowering profusely and many butterflies including clouded yellows flitted by. Seeing Cicely I told her about where I had seen the butterflies. Skirting the walls I found both Roger and Linda at the entrance to the complex and went in with them. Roger paid the man in the ticket office a few lie and said that another would join us for Cicely was still outside photographing butterflies.

Inside patches cultivated for crops we cut out of rough grass that spread between the ruins. The tall bell tower we had seen from below sparkled in the sunlight. It looked as if it had at least two storeys from the window openings. Other ruins presumably a former church dominated one end of the interior space. There was some information about the place in the office to a low building that the guardian probably lived in. When Cicely arrived she went over with Linda to see the rabbits that the guardian kept near to the walls. I glanced at the information then went to examine the bell tower.

A snapshot of the history of the place is as follows. Around 1930, a treasure containing 18 golden coins minted between 1050 and 1350 was found in the territory of Slimnic. Twelve of the coins were from mints located half way down the river Elba. So it can be presumed that colonists in the 14th century from the eastern part of Germany lived in the vicinity. But the Saxon community in the region goes even further back than that. The fortress at Slimnic was supposed to guard the way from Mediaş to the residence of the seat of Sibiu but hostile historical events left the fortress in the ruinous state we could see around us. The citadel was built by local serfs and was used as a defendable place in times of invasion, or conflict. The first mantle walls, built of uncut stone, were erected in the 12th century, at the time of the great Tatar invasion. The construction was modified later with brick in the 15th century to make it even stronger. And during that period the Gothic chapel at the north of the citadel was also transformed into a defensive tower. During its lifetime the citadel was besieged many times including by the Turks in 1602 and fell to invaders twice. The red brick walls preserved to date form two polygonal precincts. The southern one that encloses a well was badly damaged at the beginning on the 18th century. The tower in the northern precinct has walls up to 3.5 m thick at the base, but no battlements. During the 14th century construction of a Gothic basilica was started but was not finished. All that remains of the church today are its walls, except for the northern one, which has been destroyed. After 1717 the fortress was repaired several times. During World War I the Germans took a precious bell but later in the 1950s the bell tower, the southern walls, and the northwestern defensive tower were restored to the current state that we saw.

A cart loaded with hay

Inside of the tower was dusty and badly worn steps led up to the place where the bells hung. We were told not to ring them, as they were used for warnings to villagers for important events, or more mundanely a lunchtime bell for workers in the fields. There were three bells hanging down, one larger that the other two and small ladders were placed below the window ledges so that you could climb up and look at the village below strung out along the valley. After exploring some more and watching loaded carts of hay being driven along the stony track below the citadel's walls we left for our next destination.

Our route took us northwards along a country road passing by other villages with citadels that we didn't stop to explore such as Ruşi, Seica Mare, Kaltwasser, and Agirbiciu. From Sliminic we drove over a hill to another river valley that of the Tarnava Mare, which we followed to a more open valley at Copşa Mică. Here there were ruinous old factories looking blackened, or in a burned out state in places. It looked a most inhospitable place. The road turned to a right heading northeastwards along the valley through the dirty looking town.

According to Wikipedia Copşa Mică had a population in 2000 of 5189 that was down by 23% from its population in 1989, the year communism collapsed in Romania. The town was known for its status in the 1990s as one of the most polluted in Europe, due to the emissions from two factories in the area. A factory that was operational from 1936 to 1993, produced carbon black for dyes; its emissions permeated the area for nearly sixty years, leaving soot on homes, trees, animals, and everything else in the area. The effects from these decades of deposits are still visible today. Another source of the pollution, less visible but with even more serious effects to the health of the town's residents, was from Sometra, a smelter whose emissions have contributed to significantly higher incidence of lung disease, impotence and deformities in new born children, along with a low life expectancy, which is nine years below Romania's average.

Other sources used to try to discover why the place looked so bad yielded that Ceausescu is blamed for the pervasive and widespread environmental degradation that left many parts of Romania in situations of ecological disaster. During his rule, industrial units were situated in such a way as to concentrate pollution from industry into a few small areas, leaving the rest of the country relatively pristine. Copsa Mica had the misfortune of being designated as one of these 'special' locations, in spite of the fact that the orographic and meteorological positioning of Copşa Mică is not favorable for polluting industries. Short smokestacks kept pollution from spreading over a large area, and farmers were forced to sell only at Copşa Mică markets in order to restrict the spread of toxins through the food chain. Apparently the risk to workers was acknowledged and they were compensated with higher wages. But during this period factories deteriorated through lack of proper maintenance, exposing workers to even higher levels of toxicity as the government was retreating more and more behind a veil of secrecy.

Post communism cleanup efforts have caused widespread unemployment; 1,700 lost work with the shutdown of Carbosin in 1993, and new technology allowed Sometra to lay off 2,400 workers throughout the mid-nineties. The town's population now is mostly poor. It is said that many of the former workers look to their previous hazardous jobs longingly. The town's utilities infrastructure is also in a poor shape, as evidenced by a recent outbreak of dysentery and diarrhea caused by problems with the water network, which is controlled by Sometra.

Between 1993 and 2001, concentrations of all major pollutants decreased significantly, but Copşa Mică remains extremely polluted. In the Tarnava Mare river, downstream from Copşa Mică, even with the considerable decrease that was noticed over the last decade, the lead concentration remains more than twice the Maximum Acceptable Value (MAV), zinc almost ten times, cadmium is close to MAV, and copper is about half of MAV.

In many ways, Copsa Mica is a microcosm of Romania with regard to environmental issues. The 1999 and 2000 European Commission's regular reports criticized the Romanian government for its failure to enact policies and take action to protect the environment.

In Romania, compliance and enforcement of pollution regulations are limited by a multitude of factors, including: a lack of incentives, difficulties with public participation, a lack of technology, financial limitations, and most of all, the slow process of privatization, as well as corruption at all levels. Though Sometra, Copşa Mică's remaining factory, was privatized fairly smoothly in 1997 the new owners from the Greek firm Mytilineos Holdings were unwilling to implement many necessary environmental protection measures. The owners say that they inherited a firm riddled with problems, and only so many of them can be solved without forcing the plant to be shut down entirely. Poverty in Copşa Mică is indicative of the national situation, as 28.9% of Romania's population still remains below the poverty line.

We were glad to be away from the dirty town driving southwards from the main road through a small river valley lit with glorious sunlight. It was a perfect day and we could forget what we had seen only minutes before. We were heading towards Valea Viilor. This Romanian name for the village, means "Vineyard Valley" alluding to, no doubt, the supposedly excellent wine made by villagers. The Hungarian name, Baromlach, means "the cattle" and predates the previous name. The German name, Wurmloch, which was used half a century later, though it sounds similar to the Hungarian version has a different roughly meaning, "snake hole"; it is strange that the meaning of the place names are so different. The place is massive compared to Slimnic and has a fully intact church.

Noble families owned the land at Valea Viilor at least until 1359 when the land was mentioned as a free commune in the records. The church situated in the centre of the village was built in the 13th century in Romanic style. In the 15th and 16th centuries it was enlarged and rebuilt in Gothic style. At the same time fortifications were added, an oval precinct with 7-8 meter high mantle walls. Inside the church you can see some remains of the old church in the floor of the vestry. A protective 8m high wall 1.5m thick surrounds the church with an internal Loggia on brick arches, a solution adopted from the defensive architecture of contemporary towns. Towers were placed in the east, west, north, and south with the western one being a gate tower. The fortress of Valea Viilor is impressive and because of the sculptural character of its fortified aspects is a UNESCO World Heritage Site.

Our searches took us around the Loggia and the flower borders. The interior of the church has some Baroque aspects to it, particularly the altar, and interestingly there is a well in the centre of the church choir that provided water at times of siege. It also has some Saxon furniture dating from the 16th century. We climbed the bell tower and looked out on the village that spread along the valley. The only bell had decoration and writing upon it that I couldn't translate but suspected was some kind of dedication.

A little later drove back to the main road where we turned right and eastward further up the Tarnava Mare river valley towards the town of Medias. Arriving there found that there was a railway to cross to get to the historic centre. After a little thought turned down Strada Avran Iancu from Strada Hermann Oberth, the main street through the town and an extension of the road we arrived on, we then took a right and left to eventually drive down a town road, Strada Nicolae Lorga, into the historic Centre and parked near to some barriers across the road; from there we walked down into Piața Regele Ferdinand 1.

Loud rap music emanated from speakers surrounding a basketball court set up in the square on one side of which was a stand for spectators. Players were putting on an impressive performance to entertain the crowd. It wasn't a proper match but an impressive show of moves and scoring shots. Continuing on our tour of the old part of the town through its narrow lanes we visited the church, Biserica Evanghelică Sfânta Margareta within the fortified citadel. A feature that impressed in this extensive church was a triptych of medieval renaissance art.

Medias is an ancient town and although evidence of human presence in the area dates back to the middle Neolithic, the city was first mentioned during the Roman occupation as Per Medias (meaning the town at the crossroads). In 1283, after the Saxons settled in Transylvania, the city became Sacerdos de Medias, while in 1389, it was renamed Villa Medies. During the Middle Ages, Medias, like most other towns in Transylvania, was strongly fortified. Its 33 craft guilds built, maintained and defended the bastions of the walled city against invading forces and the fortified church of St. Margaret represented the core around which the citadel gradually developed. The center of the ancient settlement of Medias has maintained a medieval feel with narrow winding lanes, centuries-old houses and a large pedestrian square surrounded by colorful facades.

We left Medias after first taking a break at a roadside café for a sandwich then continued eastward up the valley following our planned route and stopped on the roadside at the Roma village of Brateiu where a large range of copper implements were on display many of which were large stills. These were the products of the Căldărarii Clan who are copper smiths. Away from the roadside were their houses large and partially built but with extremely ornate decorative architecture to such extremes as being seen rather over the top by our tastes, perhaps even Disneyesque. The buildings look as if they are constructed using a kit of parts to add on rooms for perhaps an extended family when required. The women were dark and attractive and dressed in traditional long colourful clothes while the men in contrast are rather somber in their black wide flat brimmed hats with a domed crown. They beckoned us to look at their wares.

Peter had told us about their way of clan life showing both allegiance and economic deference to the clan chief, the Bulibaşă. He told us the men were artisans who made cauldrons from copper, or brass, and that the women sometimes made brushes. I knew little about the Roma people and wanted to know more

The Căldărarii are coppersmiths or corturari, making fine products exclusively by hand from sheets copper, or brass. The people are very proud and despise Gypsies who have lost their identity. You enter the village Brateiu from Medias in 'Coppersmiths Street'. It is curious that almost all members of this community have the same name, Tinker or Traian with forename attached as in any other Western European name. The Corturarii say they are not Gypsies or Roma they differ even in spoken speech and say, "Our language is different from that of Gypsies, a few words are similar but when we talk, we do not understand the other Gypsies". Before 1960 the Căldărarii were nomadic living in tents. They had horses and carts and walked between camps. Under the communists they were made to live in houses and at the beginning Brateiu only had two old houses. They built new ones and extended the village when they had the resources to do so, hence what we had seen with the partial builds and what looked like extensions. Currently there are 300 families living in Brateiu and on average each family has three children. The Căldărarii boast that they can work almost any form in copper using many tiny hammer blows to turn a piece of metal into an exquisitely formed object, yet sometimes they heat or anneal objects in a călesc. The tools of their trade have remained unchanged for at least 200 years. Their work is hard and tedious, as well as dirty because of the copper oxide, which stains clothes. Among customer orders, which incidentally are taken from all over the world, are sinks and Roman amphorae. The Coppersmiths craft is taught from childhood and is in the blood. Children of 5-6 years are given hammers to hit copper on an anvil as a form of play. A test piece for a graduating apprentice coppersmith may be making an amphora shaped vase from one sheet of metal, which would take many hours of hammering. It's not surprising then that these pieces are sold for 100 lei, which is still a remarkably low price by UK standards.

Our route took us further along the valley towards distant Sighişoara passing by further fortified churches in villages along the way, but on reaching Saraşul turned off the main road to head south along a country lane. Our journey took us through an attractive narrow valley with wooded hilltops and cultivated fields below, some growing crops of maize. Parts of the hillside were a mass of yellow from the flowers of golden rod that colonized the higher old terraces. As we approached the village a fortified church dominated our view. The shear enormity of it was impressive. Roger parked the car alongside a pedestrianized park like area of the Piața Centrala.

The first documentary evidence for the village dates from 1283 and was founded sometime in the period 1224 to 1283 by Transylvanian Saxons. The village settlement quickly developed into an important market town and by 1510 Biertan supported a population of about 5,000 people. Between 1468 and the 16th century a small fortified church was constructed and developed, but after the medieval period the town declined in importance with the rise of neighboring towns, Sighișoara, Sibiu and Mediaș. By 1930 Biertan had only 2331 inhabitants of which 1228 were Transylvanian Saxons. During World War II many men were conscripted into the Romanian army and later into the Waffen-SS. After the war many Transylvanian Saxons were expelled from the region and following the collapse of Communism in 1990 more left for Germany. Today the whole commune has a population of about 3,000 and the village itself about 1,600 people. It is one of the most visited villages in Transylvania, being an historically important place for the annual reunion of Transylvanian Saxons, many of whom now live in Germany.

Biertan's truly awesome 15th-century Saxon double-walled church was the residence of the Lutheran bishop from 1572-1867. It was declared a UNESCO World Heritage site in 1993. The church sits on a hilltop in the centre of the village. The first church on the site was a gothic basilica that was subsequently demolished with only a few parts of it remaining, such as some stone vault ribs. The church today is a hall-shaped church with the main nave and two side-aisles. It was built between 1500 and 1525 and has net-shaped brick-ribbed vaults over its entire ceiling. In 1515 the craftsman Johannes Reichmuth from Sighişoara made a special door for the vestry with an intricate locking system that moved simultaneously 15 locks. The room of the vestry housed the church's treasure when there was a siege. The church grounds hold several other buildings, including a small bastion, which was famously used as a last-ditch effort to discourage couples wanting to divorce. The unhappy couple would be locked up in the bastion for two weeks with only one bed and one set of cutlery. Apparently this method was so successful that only one couple in 400 years decided to go through with their divorce. On the southern part of the upper plateau, the 'Catholic Tower' contains preserved fresco paintings from the mid-15th century. Many towers and a bastion strengthen two defense walls with the outer situated for the most part at the base of the hill and is strengthened to the west and south by two fortified towers.

It was quite a confusing place to look around but we explored the church and its many features including the intricate vestry doorway and a good triptych. Climbed up to the higher levels of the citadel and went up one of the towers to view the surroundings. We found it a rambling yet interesting place and at the end sat in one of the courtyards for a drink from the café before moving on once more.

It was too far to go back to the main road and visit Sighişoara. Looking at the map I suggested that the road we were on would eventually take us to the Hârtibaciu River Valley even though I could see a dotted line for a road marked on the map. I told Roger to drive on. It was a beautiful valley and in that afternoon's glorious sunlight particularly so. We soon reached another village, called Richişu, again with a fortified church but drove on through and soon afterwards the road ended to become a stony track, but fortunately for us in good condition. The girls in the back were enjoying the trip taking photographs when and where they could from the car windows but I think the stony track concerned them as we wound our way up the hillside through trees at times bumping on cart ruts. After about half a kilometer at last emerged onto a tarmacked ridge road and turned left along it following the road down to another valley and the village of Pelişor where yet another fortified church was seen. Continuing on down out of the hills the distant Făgăraş Mountains in the Carpathian Chain loomed across our line of vision, greyish-purple in the afternoon sunshine set off by a beautiful pastoral scene in the foreground of woods and rolling grassy fields with here and there cultivations of maize. It was one of those magical visions that will stick within all of our memories of Transylvania.

When we reached Birghiş the wide Hârtibaciu River Valley stretched out before us and we turned right following the north side of the river, higher up than the river plain where a railway also tracked. The road was exceptionally good wider than the country roads and recently resurfaced

Thinking of those steam railway enthusiasts met at Bran Castle I recalled something I had read about the history of the locale we were passing through. The narrow-gauge railway from Sibiu to Agnita when it was first built went as far as Sighişoara. The line used to cross the standard gauge on the level near to Mohu, a village station near to where we had lunch on the day we traveled from Făgăraş to Cisnădioara. Today the old narrow-gauge railway track goes under the main line to head northeast up the Hârtibaciu Valley to Agnita. Along the first few kilometers the track from Sibiu runs through the Cibinului valley as far as Mohu station and runs parallel with the main line to Braşov. Leaving Cibinului Valley the railway then follows the path of the Hârtibaciu, which has its source in the southern part of the Tarnavelor Plateau, a few kilometres away from Apold. In the 19th century two private companies constructed the railway. They were hired by local officials to build a railway to connect Sibiu with Sighisoara across some difficult terrain to provide transportation for agricultural and mineral products, as well as for people, who until that time could only travel along roads, which were often unusable. They built the railway on a narrow track because of the difficult terrain. Work began from both ends, Sibiu and Sighisoara, and met at Agnita, the main economic centre of the area, which specialized at that time in processing of animal hides. Construction started in 1896 and was completed in September 1910, including a small branch line to Vurpar. The landscape through which the railway ran is still dreamlike with woods and hills and distant mountains but the track always remained close to the turbulent river. Until the 1970s the narrow-gauge trains were steam-hauled. At the beginning the locomotives were Austrian made, but after 1923 locomotives of German manufacture hauled the trains until 1955 when Romanian built locomotives were used. A change from steam to diesel occurred in 1970 with steam engines used only during the cold season to generate heat for the carriages, or occasionally to haul vintage trains for enthusiasts. The line remained operational from Sighisoara to Sibiu until 1965, when the section between Sighisoara and Agnita was decommissioned. Unfortunately, the final section of the Sibiu to Agnita Railway was also closed in 2001 but there is a proposed restoration

The good section of road didn't last long for not too far from the outskirts of Sibiu the road surface was stripped back to bare uneven rough stone. Maintenance work was still ongoing but there was little sign of it happening being a weekend. It was about a couple of kilometers before we drove along the old road surface again and reached the raised section of Route 1, in its motorway form, that bypasses Sibiu. We took a ramp up to it and headed south to take a down ramp to head towards Cisnãdie, which has the Saxon name of Heltau..

Roger parked the car alongside the road in a small square, the Piaţa Revolutiel, at a meeting place of country roads and close by the fortified church. The entrance to the complex was a little way up Strada Magurii. It was originally built in the 12th century as a Romanesque Basilica and was fortified during the 15th century, to protect the local population of Saxons against repeated Ottoman raids. The fortification process included double defensive walls, a moat and several defensive towers along the walls. At the same time the fortifications were done the church also had changes made to it; it was modified with a gothic architecture. We entered the main gateway to see the usual Loggia of an enclosed terrace over arches surrounding the walls. The exceptional beauty of the place was heightened by masses of white flowering hostas bordering the pathway around the walls. On entering the church I heard an organ playing and not by any normal amateur, but one more expert in the fine art of instrumental organ playing. I walked around the inside admiring the 15th century altar and a faded fresco on one of the walls and turned to explore where some excavation work was taking place with a sign saying no entry. I couldn't resist investigating and went through the tapes and climbed a ladder to the mezzanine floor where the organ loft was located. There I saw a man in his forties, I thought, concentrating on playing a particular difficult passage of music, he glanced my way with a look indicating I shouldn't be there so I beat a hasty retreat to join the others below. We left shorty afterwards to bump into what looked like a marriage procession. The bride dressed in a short black dress and a black cape followed by two colourful bridesmaids. They walked towards a car that had just arrived with a wreath of flowers on it. Taken aback by the sight of a bride in black we got in our car to drive down to the local supermarket, a Mini-Max Discount Store at the junction of 106D and 106C in the village.

After doing our shopping we drove up hill to Cisnãdioara returning to the Belvedere. Seeing Nadina we asked her to bring a carafe of red wine over to a table in the secluded courtyard area between the 'Reception' building and the upper pool area that was enclosed by high walls on the poolside with ovens set into them. When the wine arrived with a smile from Nadina the girls fetched some nuts and crisps to have with it.

Much had been seen in the day and now appreciated the area known as 'The Saxon Villages'. Perhaps they were left alone in their defensive citadels for most of the time when marauders came through from the east, as they were too small to bother about except for food and wine. But who knows what difficulties and fears they had. A little later the cook came to light up one of the barbeque ovens and later still Peter came to inspect it. We could hear the jollity coming from above at the poolside where probably the extended family and friends were having their Saturday celebrations.

Evening dinner started at seven thirty with more wine and ended three hours later. Chicken soup was served first in a large tureen with floating islands of polenta in it. The following main course though was disappointing. A slice of overcooked pork was served on plates with strong tasting sausages and mashed potatoes with a side dish of cabbage salad. Having consumed as much as we were able some very blackened mutton pieces we brought to us with a dish of raw garlic paste, which was definitely not aioli, to have with it. Nadina made up for the disappointment though by staying to talk with us. Her boyfriend of five years was helping out with serving as well as assisting in the kitchen. Our conversation ranged widely about Romania, Copşa Mică and its troubles, independence of minorities including comparison to the UK, Scotland, Ireland and Wales. We talked about women and their lot, about pensions, religion, construction and restoration work. It was a good evening heightened by the barbs thrown at me by Linda. Peter joined us for a short time too and when telling him about the bride in black he seemed quite surprised and had no explanation for it.

It had been a good day. I enjoyed the trip around the Saxon Villages and learned too a lot about the situation in Romania and the history of the region. The beauty is overwhelming but so is the poverty and shear plight of certain people locked in to polluted areas. I went to bed with many things to think about, the night warm and starry, Nadina, her boyfriend and cook smoking cigarettes on the terrace walkway outside of the kitchen as last night, as we all passed by saying our 'Goodnights'.

Transfăgărașan Road

Early Sunday morning was yet another beautiful start to the day. I had gone outside with my sketchbook. Only one other person was about who was drawing water from one of the wells in the village. Walking a little I eventually decided to sketch the tower of the church opposite the Belevedere, the Evangelische Kirche, with its square cross-section stone tower surmounted by a terracotta tiled conical roof that is formed by eight triangular panels curving down to a square cross section overhanging the tower. It was difficult to get a full view of it because of surrounding trees and the wall to the grounds so I went around the back to enter the grounds and settled down to sketch.

Unfortunately I didn't have enough time to be satisfied with my effort before I had to leave for breakfast picking Cicely up on the way. The buffet layout was the same as the day before except there was a bowl of fruit too. I asked the cook for an egg but either she didn't understand, or she forgot about it. In conversation with Nadina, who was still wearing her body hugging black tights, she told us that she was practicing company or commercial law and will be working again on Monday. She only helps out her aunt at weekends. Our plan for the day was to dive up the Transfăgărașan Road at least as far as the mountain pass.

Evangelische Kirche at Cisnãdioara

So shortly after a good breakfast we set out, driving first down through Cisnãdie to Route 1 then following it eastward up the Oltul River Valley from the roundabout junction with route 7. Route 1 had been modified according to the map I was using for the road bypassed the villages of Bradu and Avrig with their fortified churches. Soon afterwards it passed through Porumbacu de Jus where I spotted the turning we wanted, route 7c, a country road.

Driving south towards the mountains the morning still bright with the sky a clear blue we were all full of anticipation of what was to come. The surrounding farmland grew maize and potatoes and in one field there were flowering roses bunches of which were being sold at a roadside kiosk. On through the village of Cârţişoara the road was straight and lined with tall poplars full of bunches of green mistletoe. The blue-green mountains loomed even closer and soon we were climbing up through thick woods of conifer the road twisting and turning as it gained elevation. At times shear cliff faces of bare rock rose above us, but trees now blocked our view from anything but our immediate surroundings. It was not long afterwards that we approached the busy tourist spot of 'Balea Cascada', the waterfall sightseeing area and cable car station, but we didn't stop and continued on around a hairpin bend up through the woods having only driven 21km from the Route 1 intersection.

The Transfăgăraşan is called 'The Way of the Clouds' and is the highest road in Romania. It ascends to 2,034m at the pass and runs north to south across the highest part of the Carpathian Mountain Chain between the highest peaks in the country, Mount Moldoveanu (2544m), and Mount Negoiu (2536m) and connects the region of Transylvania with Wallachia, rising from 1034m to 2034m in only 30 km. The road was built for military purposes between 1970 and 1974 on the orders of the Romanian dictator, Nicolae Ceausescu. One of the most difficult sections is said to be on the north side of the mountains between Balea Cascada and Lake Balea a distance of 13 km. From Balea Lake the road passes through Goat Tunnel, which is 887m long, to the south side of the mountains and is the longest tunnel in Romania. It height is 4.4m and width 6m with a 1m sidewalk and it's neither lit, nor has any artificial airflow. On exiting on the south side the road winds steeply down to Cascada Capra.

On the journey upwards we stopped several times to look through gaps in the trees to the river gorge. Further on, becoming clear of trees, we looked up and down the glacial valley through which the road snaked. Cicely and myself had driven on more frightening roads in France and I am sure Roger had too but nevertheless it was a fine road and I think Roger was enjoying himself nevertheless. The view to the north was of the upper glacial valley and beyond it the Transylvanian plateau marked on the horizon by a distinct boundary inversion layer that we had now climbed above. Driving on to the pass we came across a collection of roadside stalls selling food and tourist trinkets and a car park just beyond them. Roger drove down into a flattened area of rough stone to leave the car.

East of the road was a set of portable toilets with a woman collecting money outside. I think she should have paid me to go inside for the experience was not pleasant everywhere covered in human excrement. Relieving myself I got out as quickly as I could. Just over from the stalls down in a hollow was Balea Lake a clear open stretch of water surrounded by mountain peaks that were reflected in its smooth surface. A few people stood on small islands off the end of a spur of land. It was a weekend and the place had a busy holiday atmosphere. Over in the far northeastern corner of the lake a building with an outdoor terrace suspended above the water looked an inviting restaurant. We made our way over to it passing by many alpine flowers still in full bloom. Unfortunately when we got there found that there were no free tables. A joyous crowd was eating lunch served in both the dining room and on the outside terrace. From the terrace we looked out on the mountains and the clear lake with myriads of small fish swimming in it. Sadly leaving the festivities of lunch walked back up to stalls at the roadside that catered for all manner of foods, cheeses, air-dried hams, boiled corn on the cob, cooked balls of polenta, baskets of soft fruit and numerous other things. Linda bought some cheese and bread for our lunch and also a Kürtöskalács, the spiral dough bread.

Roger drove the car further down out of the main car parking area to park off a track on grass by a little mountain stream. There must have been a few hundred people at Balea Lake having fun and picnics. I spotted a bride and her groom being photographed by the stream and went over to take some photographs. She wore an unfathomable dress if you can call it that. It was white of course with an off the shoulder bodice and fluffy long knickers, which I suppose you could call shorts for they were down to just above her chunky knees. This white fluffiness I first thought were feathers but on a closer look was gathered cotton or silk tulle. She also wore a long skirt with a slight train at the back but open at the front in the same soft downy material. The overall effect was pleasing to the eye. The official photographer forced the bride and groom into different positions for his idea of the best photographic effect and told them to move off down stream. She only wore flat open shoes exposing her toes but she didn't seem to mind scrambling over the sharp rocks. I took a few more photographs from above at a pool where she changed her shoes into high heels.

Mount Negoiu

We stood by the open boot of our car munching bread and cheese watching other people coming in to find parking places or having their picnics. Up towards the pass a catenary wire had been set up between two rocky outcrops about 100m apart. The highest one was over towards Balea Lake, a few people queued up to use it. It was interesting for a time to watch the antics of the various people sliding down the wire over the chasm below them to be caught by a man at the other end. There were screams of course and showing off by young men, but it was all good fun. I unfortunately missed the bride I had photographed earlier going on it, Linda told me about it later. I had moved off to a rocky outcrop to do some sketching of the peaks below Mount Negoiu. The shifting shadows as cloud moved across the landscape made drawing difficult so the end result wasn't to my liking.

A little later we were on the road again driving through the tunnel to the south side of the mountains. On emerging from the tunnel looked out on to a steeply descending landscape. A wooded valley was far below us, probably the headwaters of the Argeşul River that would eventually flow down to the Danube many miles to the south. A little way down the road Roger stopped the car. Below I could see a flock of sheep crossing the road holding up the traffic, we decided to go and investigate. Driving further down the mountainside we stopped again at the roadside to watch shepherds and their dogs.

Calm and dignified are words you would use to describe both the shepherds and their dogs that live and work with their flocks of sheep in Romania. They have evolved over the centuries to cope with the harsh climate and rugged environment looking after vast flocks that wander freely across the mountain pastures. Similar dogs, we had seen in the Bucegi Mountains above Sinaia. They are descended from breeds that originated in the Carpathian Mountains called the Mioritic sheep dog. They are large dogs that have an inbred instinct to protect their owners. Romanian shepherds harness this instinct by rearing the dogs from pups along with young lambs and this way a dog grows up believing that it belongs to the sheep and is left to roam freely with the flock. Anything that threatens the flock will immediately trigger natural responses to protect them for these dogs are a formidable and absolutely fearless when it comes to predators. Any wolf, bear or lynx that threatens the flock will be challenged by barks and if this fails to see off the threat the dog will attack. The Carpathian Mountains are a wild area and more than a third of the world's bears, wolves and lynx roam this landscape. But people too must beware of the dogs for if you get too close to the flock you could be treated as a predator. In the part of the country we were in we were privileged to see a system that is almost extinct in Europe known as transhumance and pendulation. This involves the movement of flocks between the lowland plains and the mountain ranges to take advantage of seasonal changes. The practice was once common but is now confined, in any significant way, to Romania. Sadly though, the pressure to adopt more intensive farming methods and meet EU regulations will see an end to this way of life in a few years.

Three shepherds stood at the roadside chatting to a man in a car whom we had seen earlier taking photographs of the flocks. The shepherd's had long poles that they used as a walking stick and wore black felt hats called pălărie din fetru with a very narrow brim. These hard felt hats are made by artisans in specialized workshops and are worn throughout the year. The style varies widely in shape and size of brim according to area. The wide brimmed hat appeared around 17th-19th Century and felt hats with broad brims up to 60cm were worn in 19th & early 20th century, and continued to be worn in Valea Bistriței, Moldavia until 1940s. Hats with 40cm brims were worn in central Transylvania and Muntenia. Felt hats with hard upturned brims - cu găng - were worn in Crişana, Hunedoara and Bucovina following a fashion of the gentry. Wide brimmed felt hats with a large peacock feather (Roată de păun) are still worn in Năsăud, further south hats are much reduced in size, shepherds along the Carpathians wear felt hats with very small brims, as the present day fashion is to do away with the brim altogether.

Shepherd and sheep passing down the mountain

It was a magnificent sight in a spectacular landscape the sheep always moving but not rushed and the dogs sitting looking or walking slowly behind them. The shepherds drove onwards downhill always taking a gentle descent by spiraling around a hill to the valley below. Roger drove us further down into the valley to get a better view of the event taking place and eventually we saw them crossing the roadway far down below us kicking up clouds of dust as they rushed down a bank onto the road holding up cars travelling on it. The sheep were in good condition from their summer on the high pastures and were well looked after and were a credit to the shepherds.

We drove back up over the pass through the tunnel the Balea Lake area, still with crowds of happy people enjoying the afternoon sunshine in magnificent surroundings. There was not much traffic to contend with and we were back at the Belvedere by five. Roger seemed tired after the journey and we agreed to meet up at seven in the courtyard area for wine and nibbles, it had been a great day.

Rested from our successful day's outing I ordered a litre of red wine from Nadina, who was still in her black tights and short top. I had been going over our future plans since getting back from the mountains and measured the distances once again. I thought it would be a very long journey to Guru Humorului and was going to suggest that we break the journey at the town Gheorghie that according to the Lonely Planet Guide had a few hotels, or the nearby village of Lazarea just north of Gheoghie that had several guesthouses. By changing the plan we would be able to visit Sighişoara on the way that I knew the others would support. When Roger arrived he wanted a beer not wine and Cicely wanted a coke that left Linda and I to drink the wine between us. I put the new plan to Roger and he agreed wholeheartedly and saw the sense of stopping half way for one night because there would be many driving hours. We relaxed and talked about the day and the fine sights we had seen. Peter came over seeing the maps on the table. I told him that we had been going over the route for the next day. He glanced at it and made a couple of suggestions that altered the route a little. These were to visit Corund where they had many potteries and another village where they had basket weaving. In conversation he told us that he had built the Belvedere himself and what we saw was all relatively new.

A little later Nadina came to tell us that the soup was ready so we went on through the reception building to the dining room. Stella was there too and told us that the soup Ciorba De Burta was made from cow belly. It was much like chicken soup and had slivers of white meat floating in it and not at all like the tripe dishes served in England. I liked it and had a second helping. The main course was stuffed peppers. They were stuffed with a mixture of rice and minced pork and were cooked in a tomato and pepper based sauce. It was good. Afterwards I had a coffee and Stella brought out two jars of blackberry jam for Cicely and Linda that she had made from the berries collected by the Gypsies. A little later Nadina brought out our bill for she, Stella or Peter would not be there in the morning as they were all due at work. Stella worked as a financial director at the council in Cisnãdie, Peter worked for a Civil Engineering Company and Nadina in law office in Sibiu. When we paid the bill we gave Nadina a little extra and she expressed thanks with kisses all round.

After dinner taking a walk around the village in bright moonlight from an almost full moon we found the evening was still warm from the day's heat. A little later returning to the Belvedere we heard a voice speaking in English call out to us from one of the top windows of a house by the square. A young woman asked if we were English and discovering we were invited us in saying "I have a secret to show you."

At iron entrance gates two dogs came out wagging their tails and barking, then she arrived to open the gates and ushered us in to the house and on into a room that was obviously a bar. There she offered us drinks of the local hooch with a bilberry flavor. The secret she had to show us was her B&B with activities that are promoted by Trip Advisor. The name of their company is 'Secret Transylvania' and besides having accommodation to offer in two village houses they have converted they also organize activities for photography, horse riding, hay cart rides, mountain biking, bear and lynx watching, bird watching and general nature studies and are also will be arranging a painting course. Apparently Diana came to Romania twelve years ago originally arriving to work in an orphanage as a qualified social worker gained through her university degree. Her partner, Jeremy, came in while we were drinking with two guests from the UK. Diana and Jeremy had set up their company together four years previously.

I had read about the orphanage at Cisnãdie, which is situated on a three hectares plot of land above Cisnãdie and is the SOS Children's Village, officially opened in 1993. The family houses are built in the local rural style, using both natural stone and wood. Six family houses are grouped around a playground, and the other six around an old tree and have a capacity for 72 children. It also accommodates the village director, SOS aunts (who support the SOS mothers and take care of the children when the mothers are on leave), and an administration and service area. The SOS Nursery consists of four group rooms, a multi-purpose room, a room for medical treatment and a playground. It can accommodate up to 100 children and became operational in 1995. When the children reach adolescence they meet their special needs through a SOS Youth Facility that was set up in Sibiu in 2001. The youngsters can stay there during their vocational training, or higher education, and prepare themselves for an independent life. The SOS Social Centre runs two facilities: a holiday camp for up to 30 children from all over Romania and a family-strengthening programme. This programme offers access to essential services for child development (eg. educational, nutritional and health support, social skills) and supports families to protect and care for their children. It also aims to link families with income generating activities and offers them help to improve parenting skills. Moreover, it provides support for education in state schools and nurseries by way of materials, hygiene, cleaning materials and breakfast for the children.

We talked about what she and Jeremy thought of Romania. They said it was difficult to get things done and that there was corruption in public services. They gave us some examples to think about, such as the village we were in that still uses well water, as do many others in Transylvania. An EU grant is available to put in piped water but the local council in Cisnãdie couldn't match the grant money and had to abandon the idea.

The same council also said that they could no longer collect Cisnădioara's rubbish even though the village pays all of its taxes. We talked about construction projects and she said that they had had difficulties but Stella at the Belvedere didn't have any when they were building implying that there was corruption at the town hall. Incidentally the Belvedere takes the overflow from them. And they only charge 100 lei per night for B&B, cheaper than the Belvedere. We went on to talk about their various activities it all seemed good and we wished them well when we took our leave. Before going she said take a look in the old fire station to see something interesting. Walking back in the bright moonlight we thought about what had been said and our journey the next day.

Monday dawned with the sky so clear and blue you wanted to fly. Breakfast again by eight with a full buffet this time including scrambled egg and bacon and served by the cook, who also brought out luscious slices of ripe watermelon. After breakfast I walked around the village to find a post box to post a card. I had to go over the other side of the stream that flowed through the main area of the village. At the same time I looked for the old fire station, which Diana said to look at the night before. When I found it I peered through broken glass of a dirty window at a collection of ancient looking fire fighting equipment that hadn't been used for many a year.

Sighişoara

It was another glorious day when we left Cisnădioara and reasonably early for us. Down hill to Cisnădie going through it to Route 1, the mountains clear and blue-grey and the landscape before them already peppered with people working in the fields and with several horse drawn carts out and about. Our route to the northeast was to go by way of the one followed when we toured the Saxon Villages. The traffic was almost non existent after we passed through Sibiu looking out at our pleasant but now familiar surroundings, passing through Slimnic, Seica Mare and then on through dirty Copsa Micã and busy Medias to stop briefly alongside the road at Brateiu. Cicely wanted to take some photographs of the Căldărarii and had given me some small notes of lei to pay the men. I walked with her back down to where the copper wares were on display and where two bearded elders sat in the shade of a wooden fence, a younger man with a much smaller beard stood nearby. They looked at us with impassive faces their strong blue eyes intense. I indicated to the men that Cicely wanted to take photographs of them and offered them a couple of lei, eight other 1 lei notes remained in my shirt pocket. The senior of them indicated that they wanted more and that we must pay for the two of them. In the end I gave them seven lei and they seemed satisfied with this but another bearded man came over from his copper pots indicating he wanted some, saying beer, to which the younger man joined in. The older of the two that wanted money touched his fingers to his lips aggressively but the boss still sitting waved him away. While Cicely attempted to take their photographs I went to look more carefully at their work pieces that looked quite exceptional considering it is all made by hammering. Cicely didn't take long for she was uncomfortable with the emotionless faces turned towards her.

Căldărarii Elders

Roger drove off leaving the ethnic marvel of Brateiu behind, heading next for Sighişoara. Sighişoara is one of seven fortified Saxon cities in Transylvania, known as 'Siebenburgen'. The others are Brasov (Kronstadt), Cluj (Klausenburg), Sibiu (Hermannstadt), Bistrita (Bistritz) Medias (Mediasch), and Sebes (Mühlbach).

According to legend in 1284 the lost children of Hamelin emerged from the 'Almasch' (Varghis) cave in

88

Transylvania, which is just to the north of Baraolt. They were lured there by the magical tune of the 'Pied Piper', a Romany, who had been cheated by burghers after ridding them of their plague of rats. This of course is the romantic explanation for the presence in Transylvania of Germans following ancient customs, yet isolated by hundreds of kilometers from Germany. The reality, as we found out on our tour of the Saxon Villages, is that the fortified towns and villages of Transylvania were established in the 12th Century by settlers from the Moselle region, referred to locally as Saxons. They were attracted to Transylvania initially by Hungarian rulers who wanted them to guard mountain passes against Tatar and Ottoman raiders. They created the 'Siebenbürgen', the seven fortified cities and in the villages they constructed fortified churches in which inhabitants could shelter in times of war and siege.

Sighişoara was a Dacian settlement. In the third century BC it was known as known as Sandova but from the second century AD it was an Imperial Roman Castrum, a base for the fighting legions, but no evidence of these ancient settlements remains today. Probably the earliest German community was established as a village with a fortified refuge on the Castle Hill but was destroyed by a Tatar invasion in 1241. Shortly afterwards it was rebuilt and the Dominicans in 1289 took interest in it as a place for a monastery and other German colonists, mainly craftsmen, followed in their wake in the 14th century. The town was fortified with curtain walls and towers surrounding the hill because Ottoman invasions were a continual threat. Later, in the 15th century the defenses were reinforced with walls

15m high with 14 defensive towers, but today only nine towers remain. During the town's expansion it played both an important strategic, as well as a commercial role, and became one of the most important towns of Transylvania with German artisans and craftsmen dominating the urban economy. The Wallachian prince Vlad Tepes, Vlad Dracul's son, was born in the citadel in 1431. His father minted coins in the town and issued the first document with the town's Romanian name, Sighişoara.

We approached Sighişoara from the west via the Strada Corneşti keeping the River Tărnava Mara to our left. It was impressive, the old town high on a hill to our right dominating the surroundings. We followed the contours around along the Strada Morii looking for a way up and parked the car opposite the Tourist Information Centre in Piaţa Octavian Goga. The girl in the Tourist Office spoke good English and I asked her whether we could drive a car to the old town. She said yes we could if we go on further around we would see a road up to it. I left with a town map she had given me. Roger drove off to Piaţa Hermann Oberth where there was a little park and a few restaurants; it was a scene of much activity with lots of people strolling around in the sunshine. By the side of the park a road ran up the hill, which Roger took in his head to drive up.

Stradeta Turnului was a steep narrow lane but after 150m or so we saw barriers across the road before the clock tower and could go no further and being difficult to turn around Roger turned left around a tight hairpin bend to go down the even narrower Stradeta Cetăţii, intending to take us back down to the square again.

90

Unfortunately for us a small lorry plus a trailer collecting rubbish from bins turned the corner from the square to drive up towards us. Two of the guys who were collecting bins at the roadside waved for us to back up but Roger was having none of it and switched off the engine and got out of the car. He said to them in loud English waving his hand and pointing to his eyes, "I can't back up, I'm blind". There was a stand off but although the lorry driver looked like he was going to back up gesticulations and expletives from the collection guys stopped him. I got out of the car and Roger got back in and started reversing up the hill with me guiding him. It was very difficult with steps jutting out from the houses, as well as bins in the street. Slipping the clutch caused it to burn and the smoke and the smell and fumes became overpowering. Eventually he reached the top in a cloud of gases and smoke and eased over to one side, but when the men came up collecting the bins they insisted he back up off the road because the lorry couldn't get by, fortunately for us there was a gateway to one of the houses to do so. When they eventually drove on there was no thanks given. Roger seemed relived though, but the clutch still smelled awful.

Having reached the square again without any further trouble we drove on around the citadel rock to find a way up. There was an area above us that had a large number of trees, which turned out to be a cemetery. A road called the Strada Ilarie Chendi cut up hill at the side of the cemetery wall and we followed it around to Strada Anton Pann to find a road that ramped up hill to our right. It had a ticket barrier and we had to pay 15 lei to enter. A pavé road took us on upwards to a 15th century gateway, the Turnal Croitorilor, with two arches. Passing through it we drove on to a pedestrianized square, the Piața Cetății. In a smaller square defined by flowers contained in large planters a few people sat outside of cafés. But Roger turned right along the Strada Scolii to park in a space by a hotel after which we crossed the pavé to where there were tables outside of a pensuinea café. Drinks came quickly. I sipped my iced-coffee watching two young women carrying large bunches of flowers. Cicely said she saw on TV that it was the first day back to school and traditionally the children at some schools gave flowers to the their teachers, quite a lovely idea that might improve things in the UK.

Having relaxed a little we set off to explore the town the girls sticking together and Roger and I splitting up. First of all I went down to the Clock tower off the Piața Muzeului passing by Casa Vlad Dracul and Casa Venețianã both fine old three-storey houses. The Clock Tower, Turnul cu Ceas, is an important feature in the town. In fact it is the most impressive and picturesque of the nine towers. Its original role was the main gateway into the citadel and was also used to accommodate the town's council. Built in the second half of the 14th century it was modified and raised further in height to 64m in the 16th century. After a fire in 1676, caused by an explosion in the town's gunpowder store, the roof of the tower was restored to the current ornate Baroque shape that was further embellished in 1894 by colorful tiles. The four small corner turrets indicated that the town had judicial autonomy with the 'right of sword', which was the right to convict criminals to death. In the 17th century the clock was installed with a wooden horologe, which was remade in 1648 by Johann Kirschel. He equipped the clock with two large dials, one for each façade of the tower and with two groups of wooden figurines arranged in niches, the figurines being activated by the clock's mechanism. On the clock's citadel side the Goddess of Peace holds an olive branch and by her side a drummer beats the hours on his bronze drum. Above them there are the Goddess of Fairness holding a balance and the Goddess of Justice with a spade accompanied by two angels representing day and night. At 6 am the angel symbolizing the day comes out, marking the beginning of the working day and at 6 pm the angel symbolizing the night comes out carrying two burning candles in his hands marking the end of the working day and the arrival of the evening. While I looked I saw no movement of the figures, or at any other time I passed by whilst in Sighişoara.

I went back up to the street to where we had parked the car and had a look at the top end of it where the Scara Acoperită ascended to the Church-on-the-Hill, which is a gothic building that in time replaced the original fortress in building operations between 1345 and 1525. The staircase is next to School Street and is a covered wooden stairway named the 'Covered Stairs' or 'Schoolboys' Stairs' in English translations. It was built in 1642 to assist children on their way to the School on the Hill, as well as churchgoers' on their way to and from church during inclement weather. Originally the stairs had 300 steps, but today their number has been reduced to 175. I didn't go up the steps but Roger told me later that he did, instead I walked back to the clock tower and passed through the arched gateway to descend to the lower town looking at the same time to the reverse side of the clock.

On the lower town side of the clock there is a second niche holding a figurine, which is said to represent an executioner as well a second drummer. Above them there are seven figurines representing pagan gods who represent the days of the week, Diana, Mars, Mercury, Jupiter, Venus, Saturn and the Sun. These figurines sit on a rotating disk that turns at midnight marking a change of day. The clock mechanisms are still supposed to work. Restoration in 1906 was brought up to date with an electric motor in 1964.

Disappointed that I saw no movement of the figures I carried on down the narrow pavé lane passing by a loggia, a covered walkway, possibly for use in winter time. It was constructed with wooden beams with a tiled sloping roof set against a stone wall. Both the lane and the loggia walkway led down to an old house built across the passage with an archway under it for access. Going through it I reached the road Roger had driven up earlier before his 'clutch-burning-spree' and carried on down it to emerge at brightly decorated restaurants, with pots of red pelargoniums outside, into Piața Hermann Oberth. Many people were lunching and others outside were gathered in a small park area having an al fresco lunch break from their daily work. The sky was still clear and intensely blue with the air temperature probably in the upper twenties. I walked over to the main road keeping in the shade as much as

94

possible and made my way down Strada Decembrie 1918 to a money exchange to get more lei. The rate was excellent at 4.9 to the GB Pound. After exchanging some money walked through into Piata Octavian Goga then walked a little way up Strada Morii where I stood in the shade by a shop doorway looking at the town map. Castle Hill and Turnul Cositorarilor sticking out above the trees were bathed in sunlight. In English it is called the Tinker's Tower and canon ball damage is still visible in the walls, further up on top I could see the slit windows of the fusiliers' gallery. The Turnul Tăbăcarilor, or Tanners' Tower in English, was further around the walls and is one of the oldest towers. It was built to protect the main gate's interior court. As I was looking at the map to see an alternative way back up the hill to the old town I felt a tap on my shoulder and turned to see Linda there with Cicely not too far behind. They had been trying to find Roger for they couldn't contact him on his mobile. They said that they had been to a spoon-maker in the street that led down to the Clock Tower from the old town's main square. Cicely wanted to buy some spoons and needed some notes. Giving her a few hundred Lei I said I was going further up the street to some steps to see other monuments, they said they would follow.

The steps were just a short way up the road towards the square with the tourist office we had been to earlier. They rose sharply at first on ascending the hill but then turned sharply left almost parallel to the contours yet still below the town walls. Eventually a stair alley led to the base of Turnal Fierarilor, The Blacksmith's Tower. This was built in 1631 in place of the Old Barber's Tower and is built on a rectangular plan. It appears quite tall and large from the outside but inside the walls are lower compared to others. I turned right to follow a path below the walls while the girls whom had followed me so far left me and carried on towards the Clock Tower to buy their spoons.

Sighişoara from the Lower Town

I carried on around the walls looking for an opening in them. Below me through trees surrounding the citadel a patchwork of reddish-brown town roofs spread out with glimpses of the River Tărnava Mare beyond. Eventually travelling to the northeast side of the hill in an anticlockwise direction I came to an opening that entered the grounds of Sf. Iosif, a Roman Catholic Church that was built in 1894 on a demolition site of a Franciscan monastery. To the right of the church was a small park area and down from it the Turnal Cizmarilor, The Shoemakers Tower. This tower has had several reconstructions the latest in 1681 when it was rebuilt under the influence of Baroque architecture. Originally the front of the tower was an artillery bastion but this was demolished in 1846. The tower has a pointed spire shaped roof and a covered outside staircase leads to the second floor. Crossing over one of the old town's narrow roads I walked down Strada Tâmplarilor towards the centre passing by a mixture of single and two-storey colourful townhouses. Their walls were washed in various pastel colours of green, pink and yellows. On reaching Strada Zidul Cetăţii to my right was the town's large 14th century gateway, Turnal Croitorarilor, the Tailors' Tower that we had driven in through earlier. I turned left to the Piaţa Cetăţii where I met Roger in the square. He had been up on the hill through the covered staircase and guessed that I had gone down into the lower town to get some money. The girls were still buying spoons so I went down to them to see how they were getting on.

Mark Tudose is a wood carver extraordinaire he claims. He likes to tell a story and his wooden spoons have many stories to tell. His great idea is to make an apparently simple object valuable through its story and the symbols behind the story. In life, he says, *"people search consciously or unconsciously, for just a few simple things: love, happiness, luck, wisdom; with my spoons, I am telling Romanian folk tales which deal with these spiritual elements. Among my spoons you will find the spoon of luck, the spoon of lovers, the spoon of the good and the evil and so on."* Asking him why spoons? He says, *"I wanted to work with spoons because it's a craft 100% Romanian and because there are so many designs to serve me as inspiration. For example, did you know that Romania has the largest collection of wooden spoons in the world? You can see over 5,300 models at the Wooden Spoons Museum (Muzeul Lingurilor de lemn - Ion Tugui) in Campulung Moldovenesc. It's a fascinating thing to see, really."* Mark learnt this traditional Romanian trade from his grandfather and Mark's family are all wood carvers, including his mother and his sisters. Throughout the year, he travels with his spoons to craft fairs all around the country. The girls were lucky to find him on the streets of Sighişoara, his adoptive city he likes so much. He first visited Sighişoara in 2005. *"It was love at first sight,"* he says. So, he decided to leave behind the capital city of Bucharest to live in the place of my dreams.

Cicely had bought the Power Spoon and the Luck Spoon and his story behind these is as follows.

The snake is a power symbol but at the same time known as the protector spirit of the house, or "the one who defends the citadel's gates" Also the flag of the Dacian people used to be represented by a snake (or dragon). Its head was made of iron, and the rest made of leather. This way, when the wind blew into the dragon's mouth, it would sound like a wolf howling, which would discourage the enemy and scare any horses that weren't used to the sound.

The stork is a luck symbol. In Romanian folk tradition they used to say that when a stork makes her nest on a house she protects it from fire, water and thieves.

98

I got the girls to follow me up School Street to a shop on the left-hand-side at the top, near to the covered stair, where I wanted to show them some of the traditional garments and a shop selling all types of things. It was in the latter shop that Cicely bought a doll for our great niece Emilia. After they had explored the shops and some of the attractive yards at the back we returned to Roger who was standing by the car. He had been looking at a menu displayed on the outside of Hotel Sighişoara that was decked out with baskets of red pelargoniums. He had also had a look around the place and suggested we had a snack lunch there. It seemed a great idea to us all, so we went in.

 The place dates back to the 16th century and looked attractive and out back was a large patio area with pergolas covered in ivy that shaded wooden tables laid with white tablecloths. We sat at one pondering on the contents of the menu while we ordered drinks; I had an iced coke. At first there seemed to be no agreement on what we should have for we couldn't just get one plate of mixed things for the waiter said it wasn't possible so three of us decided on a plate of 'Caprese' to share, Roger opted out he wanted a main vegetarian course with frites. Thinking that one Caprese wouldn't be enough we ordered two. However, when our orders arrived each Caprese had 4 Bruschettas and in the middle of the large plate thick slices of beefy tomatoes alternating in stack form with thick slabs of cheese, six pieces in all, so two plates were quite ambitious for a snack lunch. But thinking our plates were a challenge I only had to look at Roger's enormous selection and quantity on an extremely large plate making our offering shrink into insignificance. His plate had Macedonian salad, aubergine fritters, courgette fritters, boiled potatoes, cauliflower, broccoli and slices of cucumber and tomato. In the end we finished one and a half plates of Caprese but Roger's plate had hardly been attacked even though Linda helped him out little it was a mass of uneaten food. Throughout the meal we caught parts of a conversation on an adjacent table that had a large Romanian family but others, judging by their accents, were American, possibly expats, for it was a celebratory meal of some sort where different dishes were passed to children and adults alike.

We left Sighişoara heading eastwards, it had been a good visit but we could have done with more time, possibly a night and another half day to see all the sites. It was indeed a beautiful old town and was obviously well cared for.

Through the Székely Area to Emma Pap

Drove eastward from the beautiful Town of Sighişoara in the 'Saxon' area passing through Securesc where woven baskets were displayed for sale at the roadside. I told Roger to take a road that I had not planned for but this proved to be a short cut and took us though an attractive part of the countryside that was off the beaten track passing through a small village of Cobăteşti. I had made the mistake because the village names weren't the same as on my map, they were all in Hungarian, so it was like driving through a strange country for this was Székely country, Harghita County.

The Székely people are among the oldest cultures to inhabit the Carpathian Basin. The origin of the Székelys is fascinating, but is a matter of some historical controversy. Traditional scholarly accounts of the Székely origins state that they were Huns, who later adopted the Hungarian language (Magyar), but other Scholars believe that the Székelys were a contingent of Hungarians, that accompanied Attila to the Carpathian Basin. Recent archaeological finds amongst the Ugar people in Eastern Turkestan seem to give credence to ancient Magyar legends, which state that the Magyars are direct descendants of the Huns. The local people have many legends about their own origin and believe that after Attila died and his empire disintegrated, Attila's youngest and favourite son Ernak (Prince Csaba), led them to safety in Transylvania before returning to the east. Ernak did indeed take the main body of Huns back to Scythia, but to a region between the Black Sea and Caspian Sea where the remaining Hunnic peoples, merged with the ancestors of the Magyars. This Hun-Magyar connection is also remembered in one of the famous Hungarian folk tales, 'The Legend of the White Stag'. The legend describes how the two sons of Nimrod, Hunor and Magor, chased a white stag into a new land and there they married daughters of the king. The descendants of Hunor became the Huns, while the descendants of Magor became the Magyars.

Eventually we headed northwards through heavily wooded country. Many horses and carts were on the road slowing us down to their gentle pace, Roger became frustrated, but it wasn't long before we reached Korund where roadside stalls and shops sold ceramics, as well as trading in traditional costumes, carpets and woven baskets; it was a prosperous looking artisan place.

Korund potters are best known for their famous blue-and-white designs, which they have been creating since the 1700s and the main products are pots, pans, vases, candleholders, and cups. Ornamental plates are beautifully decorated with a variety of symbols, such as wedge, peafowl eye, and chessboard. There is a saying in Korund: "*since the world existed they have always produced pottery*". The Szkéler women say, '*The best corn porridge can only be made in vessels made in Korund'.*

Both Cicely and Linda browsed the shops and stalls, each buying examples of the Blue and White designs with animals and flowers that appealed to them. There was no time to linger though and we set off northwards again via Plaid eventually climbing along a country road eastward through thickly wooded terrain, our destination still 50km away. It was a rough ride crossing hills and through a pass at 1287m for the road surface was in an appalling state with many potholes and damage from road slippage. It was after five o'clock when we eventually reached the town of Gheorgheni.

The town or hotels didn't look appealing to us so we drove north along the road to Topliţa hoping to find accommodation in the village of Lăzarea, (Gyergyoószárhegy in Hungarian) 6km away. Our guidebook showed 20 Pensiunes, but on arrival we saw no evidence of any. Eventually we parked in the centre of the small village that had a large village map displayed on a notice board. We found the map next to useless, it was no help at all, for all we could determine was that a castle stood on a hill close by. Fortunately we had some telephone numbers and Roger tried one but got no response happily a second number yielded a reply.

The woman who answered had no English so Roger handed the phone to me whispering she speaks French. I don't know whether Roger thought I spoke fluent French, but I did understand some of what she was telling me. She was trying to describe how to get to her place from where we were. It seemed quite complicated turning back towards Gheorgheni and with some left and rights and down a lane. She sensed my difficulties and said that her son spoke English but he was working up at the castle and would get back to us, but she did say something about attending to it too. We were considering how to follow her instructions not knowing clearly our starting place and were about to set off when Madame turned up on a bicycle and said to me, "suivez-moi" waving her arms and smiling broadly, as I went out to greet her.

Roger, driving slowly, followed the bicycle back along the main road then off down a narrow stony track to her pensiune, named after her, 'Emma Pap'. It was a bungalow and we entered the property through a double wooden side gate following her in around to a patio area. The grounds were long and narrow with out-houses strung out down one side. Emma Pap welcomed us again and beckoned us in to her small house. She showed us two double bedrooms that smelled strongly of mothballs that were cluttered with personal objects such as photographs and ornaments. The entrance to one of the bedrooms was off the hallway while the other off a small kitchen diner where also a concertina door led to a shower and toilet room. Emma seemed a pleasant enough woman and very kindly and although the price she charged wasn't cheap we took the rooms, ours being off the hall and Roger and Linda's off the kitchen.

After the agreement she opened the main gates for Roger to drive the car in and closed the gates behind him then after putting our bags in the rooms we assembled in the kitchen where Emma placed a small carafe of Pálinka (alcoholic bilberry drink) and four glasses and asked us what time we would like dinner and breakfast. I understood from her that the village was entirely made up of Székely people. She went on to say that for dinner there would be a mushroom pasta dish for the main course following soup and asked if this was OK. We agreed and went back to our rooms to sort our cases out and open windows to let in some fresh air. A little later we all gathered at a bench along one of the outhouses talking about the day and finishing off our drinks. Emma Pap had been off on her bicycle and had come back with a bag of groceries and went to one of the outhouses to cook the meal.

Dinner was ready on time at seven thirty and she called us in to the laid out table in the small kitchen. The soup was excellent with thin pasta strands floating in it. The main course was thick slices of pork in a mushroom sauce served with macaroni and for dessert she served us slices of cake. With the meal we drank from a good bottle of red Swabian wine possibly from the Banat region, or near to the Danube wine growing area.

After dinner we sat out on the bench again watching a glorious sunset and stayed for some time in the warm air as darkness came before retiring, it had been a long day

∞

Woke to another glorious morning, Emma who must have been sleeping in the single room next to ours, had laid out a fine breakfast of slices of salami, cheese, tomato and a paste with some bread. She also asked if we would like omletă. Of course we all said yes please. As expected though the omletă was scrambled egg and I had it with slices of good beefy tomatoes. During breakfast she asked if we were going to Gheorgheni, I said yes and on through Bicaz Gorges. "Pourriez-vous me déposer quelquepar s'il-vous-plait?" I turned to Roger and said Emma would like a lift to Georgheni. We agreed that this would be OK and left to get the bags.

Before I loaded the bags in the car I looked through the 'Visitors Book' that had comments from 2008. We were the first English people to stay in that period and I wrote my comment for our stay. Looking through the other comments there was an amusing one from a Danish cyclist who wrote in English, 'Thank you for coming after me!'

Journey to Bucovina via Bicaz Gorges and Lake

When we were all loaded up Roger drove out of the gate. It turned out that Emma wanted to be dropped off in the town centre, at the hospital, which was on our way. After a short journey in to Gheorgheni we said our 'good byes and thanks' to Emma Pap and left the town along a tortuous road. It had dark steep wooded hillsides of conifers either side. After about 26km we reached the location of a resort known as Lacu Rosu ('Red Lake', or Gyilkos tó in Hungarian) at an altitude of 1256m and passed through the Bucin Mountain pass with a twisting snarl of beautiful mountain scenery. We didn't stop at Lacu Rosu, which is a thriving alpine resort that sprang up in the 1970s and is still a magnet for hikers, but carried on for we were expecting a long drive to our destination.

A bizarre forest of dead tree stumps that jut out of its murky waters induces the Red Lake's mysteriousness. A legend has it that the lake was formed through the flowing blood of a group of hapless picnickers who had the misfortune to be sitting beneath the mountain when the mountainside slid and collapsed, crushing them to death. In fact a landslide occurred in 1838, which led to a natural damming of the Bicaz River and consequently flooded the valley.

The road ran close by the river cutting through sheer 300m high limestone cliffs snaking through the contours. At one point we stopped to take photographs of a spectacular limestone peak illuminated with strong sunlight before driving on down to the narrowest part of the gorge known as the 'Neck of Hell', Gâtul Iadului. At that point the road ran beneath over hanging rocks and when we passed through it found that part of the road had slipped down into the river below leaving a chasm that was fenced off by road maintenance barriers. Not long afterwards we reached Bicaz, a small town at the confluence of the Bicaz and Bistrata Rivers. It looked a sorry place with its large overpowering asbestos plant, but we turned north following a sign to Vatra Dornei.

The narrow road climbed up out of the town through hairpin bends and woods to emerge near to the hydroelectric dam (baraj) that was built in the 1950s. The road led eastwards at first over the dam before turning northwards again following the east side of the lake called Lacu Izvorul Muntelui, or 'Mountain Spring Lake', or more commonly known as Bicaz Lake. When the lake was formed it submerged several villages and the people had to be relocated. The lake is quite substantial and covers around 30 square kilometers.

For a few kilometers we drove along its east bank high above the lake giving us good views of both lake and surrounding mountains. The landscape was peppered with woods and at other times was more agrarian with farmhouses and cultivated fields. The houses were slightly different to what we had so far experienced in Romania but their gardens were still full of colourful flowers. On reaching the far end of the lake at Poiana Teiului we stopped a roadside café at the edge of the town opposite a viaduct over which the road curved westward.

Bicaz Lake

There were no loos working in the café but we ordered our drinks of coffee, tea and chocolate and looked out on the scene below of the lake and viaduct. To one side of the road, just before the viaduct, was a collection of portable loos. One by one I think we all visited them and where outside of a one hut there was a sign stating WC where a woman sat with a collection of water bottles. After paying her 1 lei she gave you a bottle of water to wash your hands, as there was none on tap and after you had finished she flushed the loo using a much larger bottle of water.

I looked around the shop adjacent to the café while I waited for the others. It was a general store selling all manner of things but the prices seemed high, for instance a chocolate snack bar cost 5 lei, probably a sign of its remoteness.

The still glorious day lit up our surroundings, as we drove on again over the viaduct following the Bistriţa River northwestwards, the trees now showing signs of autumn colour, the wide river full of rushing white water. Mountains that rose up to our left were the Muntii Bistriţei and to our right the Muntii Stănişoarei. We passed through a number of villages where farm workers with horse drawn carts loaded with hay waved to us, as we passed by, others were hay making in neighbouring fields and cows trod casually untethered along the roadside munching herbage gathered in their jaws. Many of the villages had Hungarian names and weren't marked on our map causing me to miss the planned turning at Chiril that would have taken us over the mountains. Instead we followed the river around to the south then west to Vatra Dornei, a straggling town.

We stopped in the central part near to the river. Looking around close by we didn't find anywhere that attracted us to take lunch and even looked around a little market by the bridge over the river to see if there were any good looking cafés there but to no avail. I left the others at the south side of the bridge before I went over it to look more closely at a large building on the other side. Behind it I found a supermarket and called on the others to come on over. There we bought some bread, cheese and four bottles of 'Liptons Tea'. Roger would have preferred a sit down lunch but the girls did not concur.

With our food for lunch we drove on over the bridge following signs to Iacobeni. A short way out of town we stopped in a layby where we consumed our picnic and at the same time I looked at the information we had on guesthouse accommodation around Humorului. Roger, thinking of the evening meal, said he would prefer a good hotel with a fine à la carte menu.

Deciding on our strategy we arrived at last in Bucovina and drove on to the large town of Câmpulung Moldovenesc Roger parked up near to the Tourist Office where I asked about the painted monasteries and obtained a map from them. Then we drove on to Gura Humorului following the Moldova River valley eastwards.

The Habsburg Monarchy annexed the surrounding lands from the principality of Moldavia in 1775 that became known as Bukovina. This name was derived from a German name, die Bukowina, which was taken from the Polish form Bukowina, which in turn came from the Ukrainian word, Буковина (Bukovyna). The common Slavic form of buk means beech tree. Another

German name for the region was das Buchenland that is mostly used in romantic poetry, and means "beech land", or "the land of beech trees". Bucovina became officially part of Romania after WWI and in literary or poetic contexts, the name Țara Fagilor, "the land of beech trees", is sometimes used in Romania.

Arriving at Guru Humorului we crossed the Moldova River to its north bank and shortly afterwards turned left up a road by a Best Western Hotel that led to Mănăstirea Humorului. It was only a short way via a country lane but about half way there we had to negotiate a stream crossing for extensive repair work was taking place on a bridge. After a very brief look around viewing the prospects we returned to Guru Humorului and parked outside of the Best Western Hotel. While Roger checked out the Best Western I checked out a 4-star hotel we had passed down by the river. I found the restaurant at that hotel was now closed for the season but they did have two en-suite double rooms available for three nights that were located at the back overlooking the river. The rooms seemed comfortable enough and free from traffic noise so I said that I would get our wives to look at them. Returning to the car Roger had discovered that the Best Western didn't have any rooms available. So we drove the car around to the other hotel. As we got out of the car we could hear a loud noise from a train passing near by. The girls went in to inspect the rooms and came back disappointed, the rooms being too noisy. So it was to be Plan B, The Marion, (or my original Plan A). Roger wanted to try the Bukovina Hotel just on the outskirts of town first but found no one there on arrival. We telephoned the Marion at Mănăstirea

Humorului and a girl replied who spoke good English saying they had rooms available and gave Roger instructions how to get there.

It was five thirty when we arrived but found that the Guesthouse had no sign on it nevertheless we drove up through the gate along the drive to where a young woman came out to greet us, saying her name was Roxanne. She showed us rooms on the second floor that looked fine and pleasant. After taking our bags to the rooms we sat in the garden house at the front of the property and drank cool beers Roxanne had brought out to us. Apparently it was too late to have dinner there so we had to find somewhere else to eat for the evening, but the other nights would be fine. As we sipped our drinks we looked out at two dogs and a cat playing and were very contented to have found such a quiet spot adjacent to a church and close by the monastery we were to visit.

Back in our rooms Cicely and I unpacked, showered and changed, but meanwhile Roger not satisfied with their room raided other rooms to acquire, soap, pillows and tried another toilet out as well with a mirror on the door. By seven thirty we were all ready, the clock tower bells had rung and we could hear religious chanting. Roger said it was recorded, but I wasn't so sure. Before driving off into town we checked out the opening times of the monastery but it seemed to be already open and a brief glimpse at the church was enough to encourage us for it had impressive painted images on the outside. The evening was warm and pleasant as we drove back towards the town and on the northern outskirts drove into the car park of Pensuine Valentina that had a large restaurant and an à la carte menu.

The menu looked impressive and three of us chose trout served with white sauce and with polenta, but I ordered mixed vegetables too. Roger risked the Transylvanian pork now that he was in Bucovina. It was chunks of meat and pork sausage also served with polenta. We started though with salads, one mixed with shredded cabbage, carrot and apple that was crispy and fresh, even with the dressing, and the other made up of feta cheese with cucumber and tomato. We chose a white wine for the first course and a red, Merlot, for the main. For dessert Linda and Cicely shared pancakes served with honey and chopped nuts, while I had a pancake stuffed with chocolate served with blackcurrant ice cream and cream and Roger some deep fried bread crumb coated potato balls. The whole meal cost us 240 lei, which was exceptional value.

We drove back to the Marion tired but very happy it had been a long day.

Bucovina's Painted Churches

Tower in Mănăstirea Humorului grounds

It was another glorious morning with clear blue sky as I walked down the path to the rusty gate. The village was quiet and peaceful, Roxanne was getting two little girls (daughters of her sister) ready for school. Roxanne spoke excellent English, whereas her parents didn't; her name is of Persian origin meaning 'Magnificant Star'

115

and is used by Greeks, like the wife of Alexander the Great.

I carried on through the gates and turned right to enter a stone arched portal under a tall white bell tower with a black slate roof and entered the grounds of what I assumed to be a Lutheran church, but might have been Orthodox. The ground sloped upwards towards the church a brilliant creamy-white in the morning sunshine with a tiled spire and roof. The path cut through grasses with some flowering autumn crocus. When I reached the church I sat down on a stone bench built flush against a warm sunny wall. For the next hour I sketched the tower in the monastery grounds. During this period the church had opened for a service and people started arriving. Most passed me by, but one or two came over to see what I was doing. One of these was a man dressed in traditional clothing, I showed him my sketch and he went away smiling. It was very relaxing there and tranquil and I felt very contented and was sad to leave for breakfast at eight thirty.

In the large dining room Roxanne had arranged a buffet of omelets, tomatoes, a mashed baked aubergine and a finely chopped onion mix, plus a selection of various cheeses, salami, a basket of bread, dishes of two different muesli's, a large roll of country butter and a dish of honey; coffee was also served in a large jug.

When everyone was seated, Roxanne asked whether anyone wanted tea, then Roger asked her whether she would wash his shirts. She said yes she would do washing for all of us but we must set out any dirty clothes on the settee outside of our rooms, in the landing area. She smiled with those staggering blue

116

Circassian eyes with a navy blue anterior. I asked if she was Romanian, she said yes and both her parents were too. I had seen this eye type in Greece and they are startlingly beautiful and Roxanne was an attractive young woman anyway.

Romania and its people have the paradox of being pleasant and attractive but also having a dark side, the beggars, bad Gypsies, tumble down communist health risk factories, poor roads and a recent suspect history. I thought about the labour intensive farming, both men and women hand turning hay and loading onto those tall conical stacks, the single-track overgrown rail tracks, and people walking miles because of the lack of public transport. But I felt that we were now in an area very much on the good side. The beautiful rolling hills of Bucovina were covered in trees like a furry duvet blanketing a lumpy bed, sometimes cut with deep valleys, small inviting farms and cattle wondering freely down a road, the area has a natural beauty and simplicity. Scattered throughout the countryside are picturesque villages within a rural landscape with local folk going about their daily business; horse-drawn carts dominate the lanes, driven by radiant happy people, outdoor wells and piles of chopped wood adorn the gardens in stark contrast to the frenetic pace and way of life shaped by the modern face of city living. My mind was not on breakfast but the food was good and satisfying. I was glad we were at the Marion and not at some hotel in town.

After breakfast we walked over to the monastery by way of the church next door to enter it through a side gate that was open. A few local people were carrying bunches of herbs others carried bottles of water. The monastery church stood serene in sunlight its rounded end wall covered in painted pictures aged with time and overhung with a large sloping roof. The images told stories illustrating events and people, such as saints and kings and queens. They were all around the walls, arranged in various shapes and sizes. Often images had a gruesome side warning unbelievers, or sinners, of the fate that awaited them in full gory detail.

During our stay in the area we visited most of the impressive number of painted churches such as Humorului, on our doorstep then Voronet, Dragomirna and Sucevița. Their fine exterior and interior frescoes, have been preserved and handed down from Medievil times, and because of their uniqueness and artistic value, were added to UNESCO's World Cultural Heritage List in 1993. There is, indeed, no other place in the world where such a group of churches, with such high quality exterior frescoes, can be seen. The churches were founded, in most cases, as family burial places of princes and high nobles. Each painter, although following canonical iconography interpreted traditional images in a slightly different way. They used vivid colours like the red of Humor, the famous Voronet blue and the green-red of Sucevița. The painters, most of them unknown, described biblical stories of the earth and of heaven, scenes from the lives of the Holy Virgin and Jesus Christ, stories of man's beginnings and of life after death. The scenes were first painted on the interior walls, and then extended to the exterior. The reasons for such vast representations were both religious and moralistic: to promote Orthodoxy and to

118

educate the local peasantry who were mostly illiterate.

People moved towards Humorului church from the main gate, as prayers and responses emanated from speakers on the church, it was quite enchanting. Some people emerged accompanied by nuns dressed all in black and wearing black pillbox hats with a black hood from their coverall garment pulled over the back of it. Men and women, some dressed in traditional clothes, held limp bunches of herbs and candles to light, some others carried holy water. It was 'Holy Cross Day'.

The Heroes' Cross is a magnificent monument of Busteni just north of Sinaia. The cross was built to honor those who fought for the union of the Roman people. It was built at the request of Queen Mary, who wanted to follow her dream of building a monument to all the heroes of World War One, which could be seen from a great distance. The monument was eventually raised on the second peak of Caraimanului to be visible on the plateau. The Heroes' Cross was erected at an altitude of 2291m and the inauguration of the monument and its sanctification took place on September 14, 1928, known thereafter as 'Holy Cross Day'.

I peeped into the interior of the small church that had three rooms; the far one had a priest performing the ceremony. Some women knelt in prayer while others prostrated themselves on carpets, as the interaction between priest and congregation went on. People came and went making small signs of the cross. When there was room I went inside. In the first room frescos covered all surfaces except the floor and because of no weathering they were much brighter than those outside; archangels and seraphim were all there. At a table a nun handed out tall thin candles making notes on a piece of paper who had what. Women were still prostrating themselves, or kneeling and kissing images of saints. In the next room there were more frescos covering walls and ceiling and in the final room too where the priest was still carrying out his duties, but I didn't dwell there but only looked on at a large silver icon of the Madonna and Child Jesus with wonder.

It was High Chancellor Teodor Bubuiog that built Humor church in 1530 at the behest of Voivode Petru Rares on the site of a previous monastery. The monastery was closed in 1786 and was not re-established until 1991. It is now a small convent, served by nuns. The church, devoted to the Holy Virgin, is smaller than other churches of the painted monasteries and does not have any cupolas. Otherwise, it preserves the same traditional three-cusped conventional plan appropriate to most other painted monasteries. Humor is protected by a wooden stockade rather than a stone rampart, and lacks the characteristic spire, indicating that it was founded by a Boyar, not the ruler. The belfry with a belvedere was erected in 1641, under Vasile Lupu's rule. It is a small church, with an open porch arched on three sides. The open porch is separated from the nave by three columns connected through broken arches, which have crossed vaults. The church was one of the first in Bucovina to be painted and, along with Voronet is probably the best preserved. The master painter responsible for Humor's frescoes, which were painted in 1535, was Toma of Suceava, the most famous church painter of his time.

Outside again I caught up with the others looking at the wall paintings and when we had all gathered we left by the main gate outside of which were souvenir stalls, which the girls pondered over for a while before we collected the car and drove off towards Voronet. It wasn't difficult to find a narrow lane that took us through peaceful farming country towards wooded hills and after a few kilometers we arrived at the monastery that's surrounded by stonewalls and entered through a tower gateway.

Voronet is considered by many to be the "Sistine Chapel of the East", due to its magnificent frescoes located on the west wall. These feature an intense shade of blue, known in Romania as 'Voronet Blue'. The colour is obtained from lapis lazuli, and has been used in a unique palette alongside other colors such as the 'Titian Red' and 'Veronese Green'. An old Romanian chronicle written by Ion Neculce (1672-1745), records that Stephen the Great founded Voronet Monastery in 1488 to fulfill a pledge to the hermit Daniil, who had encouraged the ruling prince of Moldavia to cast the Turks out of Wallachia. After having won the battle against the Turks, Stephen erected Voronet in three months and 21 days on the very spot Daniil had his small wooden hermitage. It remained a working monastery until the start of Habsburg rule in 1785, and only became a religious retreat again after the fall of communism.

The walls of the church were covered in frescos that seemed much brighter and more intense than those at Humor. Names of the artists are mostly lost to us, except for that of Marcu, a master, whose name is inscribed on the left side of the entrance door. The approach taken by the painters is of reassuring folk art that depicts Moldavian people in religious imagery. For instance angels in the frescoes have faces like those of Moldavian women. Archangels blow the 'bucium', a Romanian shepherd's musical instrument similar to an alpenhorn and the souls carried to heaven are wrapped in Moldavian towels, whereas the souls doomed to eternal fire of hell wear turbans just like the Turks of the day for they were Moldavia's fiercest enemy. Inside the frescos were even more spectacular and under the dome was an image of 'Christ Pantocrator', as seen many times before on our travels in Byzantine churches. The place was very busy and the nun's, as at Humor, were giving out candles and making notes. The candles were lit in a special area on a tray placed over water under the cover of an awning. Roger said that they probably recycle the wax, which was probably true. The grounds were very pleasant with many flowers especially in the cemetery area that looked like a well-tended garden.

Our next destination was westward to the monastery at Dragomirna. Suceava, formally the capital city of the Principality of Moldavia from 1388 to 1565 and is now the county town of Bucovina. When we arrived on the outskirts we drove out of the higher hills to the plain of the Suret River that was still quite distant. The town was busy and dense with traffic trying to negotiate a way through its narrow streets. We had to circumvent the old town on the hill by going in an anticlockwise way to the south and then back towards the north. It was impossible navigating with the map we had but tended instead to follow the general flow of traffic assuming that it was going our way. I asked Roger to take certain roads aiming for villages I had marked on the map but eventually realized we were lost. There was a whole network of country roads with inadequate signs. When we reached the village of Adăncata I knew that we had gone too far and told Roger to stop. But fortunately Linda suspected that the village sign was not for the village but indicated the Commune, so we drove on and after another 100m found a sign indicating Dragomirna Monastery. A narrow lane eventually took us via the village of Mitocaşi to the monastery.

The setting for the Dragomirna Monastery is beautiful, close to a forest and next to a lake. The scholar, artist and bishop Anastasie Crimca founded it in 1609. Previous to the building of the great monastery another little church had been built in 1602. This little church is in the cemetery of the Dragomirna monastery. In 1620 the monastery was surrounded by formidable stonewalls with 11m high towers, which made the monastery appear like a fortress. A tower with a belfry was also added for the entrance to the compound.

Unfortunately for us restoration work was taking place and a lot of the walls and towers were covered in scaffolding and a notice indicating that the Ministry of Culture was involved. We parked the car in a little park on the other side of the road to the main entrance and walked through a massive main gate with an arched tunnel under its tower. A nun was on the other side collecting money for the entrance fee and we paid the usual few lei. A good deal of restoration had already taken place for a lot of the walls had been repointed with lime mortar. We couldn't see as much as we would have liked to because of the building restoration work and the museum was closed too, such a disappointment. We strolled around the grounds for a bit before departing.

We drove back to Route 2 via a newly made wide road for tourist traffic the one we should have driven in by and turned north when we reached it heading up the Suceava Valley. At Danila we took a road to the west heading for Rădăuti. Roger was getting hungry and wanted to stop there and then not feeling like driving for another ten minutes to Rădăuti. It was 2 o'clock and there didn't seem to be any café-bars around in village of Milişăuţi where we had stopped but there were some places that sold drinks. Fortunately we spotted a café that did fast food, soups, sandwiches and pizzas and parked outside of it.

We ordered two pizzas, two sandwiches and a soup and two sorts of bottled tea. The sandwich I chose turned out to be a massive soft roll filled with what tasted like spam spread with tomato sauce. Roger's soup looked the right choice, chicken with a side dish of tomato sauce and two rolls of bread. Cicely and Linda shared a large pizza. One sandwich was OK for me but two no way. Roger tried to persuade me to have some of his pizza he was going to delve into when he had finished his soup. I took a thin slice finding the bottom dough mix was uncooked, but the top was OK a mix of tomatoes and capers with bits of mushroom. In the end a lot of pizza and a sandwich roll was left, but Roger was refreshed and raring to drive off again.

The drive to Rădăuti was short, white fluffy cumulus decorated the otherwise clear sky, the afternoon warm and the town like many provincial Romanian towns had a haphazard arrangement of shops in all shapes and sizes within the confines of the regions architecture. Old stork nests decorated the tops of power cable poles and doorways to buildings had carved wooden pillars and doors. Some of the buildings were of un-rendered brick and many un-mortared with ski slope roofs. We drove on through and turned along the Sucevita road that headed west towards the mountains of the Obcina Mare. There were many more trees now and the road was lined with them too. Of the many villages passed through, Marginea was special, the car was blessed as we passed a group of young women dressed in traditional clothes who swished bunches of herbs soaked in holy water at us, laughing merrily as they did so; they were having a great day out.

It wasn't long before we reached the monastery on the far side of Sucevita and parked opposite to it. The views from there were breathtakingly magnificent with rolling wooded hills both conifer and deciduous, as well as lush green meadows. The complex looked in good condition and had high defensive stone walls with towers surrounding it. Going through the main gateway we paid the nun on duty and were faced with an impressive painted church, shaped like all the others but much larger.

Sucevița is the largest and perhaps the finest of the Bucovina monasteries. It was the last one to be built, and described as 'A Poem in Green and Light', it has thousands of painted images on a background of emerald green. The fortress legacy of these mountain monasteries is nowhere clearer than at Sucevita. Set in a beautiful green valley it is fortified like a citadel with watchtowers at its four corners. It is a square-shaped compound, surrounded by a wall of length 100 m on each side and is six-metres high with a three-metre thickness. The monastery was erected in 1581 by Gheorghe Movila, Bishop of Radauti and consecrated to the Assumption in 1584. Ieremia Movila extended the church with two open porches (to the North and to the South); he also built massive houses, thick surrounding walls and defensive towers. The legend has it that an old woman had been working there for thirty years, carrying stone in her ox wagon for the construction of the monastery. This is the reason given why a female head is carved in black stone in the monastery's yard. The fortress has a double defensive role, which consequently protected the mural paintings from serious damage, as happened with frescoes of other painted monasteries. Paintings at Sucevița are the best preserved both on the outside and on the inside. Thousands of images decorate the walls of the church; in fact they outnumber the pictures at any of the other monasteries. Yet, the Western Wall is blank. Legends say that the master artist fell off scaffolding and was killed, so it remained undecorated. The frescoes are painted in purple, red and blue against an emerald green background with plenty of gold too and have a strong narrative character, many of them representing scenes taken from 16th century daily life in Moldavia. Outside the porch, unsettling imagery depicts the Apocalypse. It displays two-headed beasts and the conventional rivers of fire. On the South wall, there is a remarkable 'Tree of Jesse' displaying both the human and divine genealogy of Jesus. A scene, 'the Prayers to the Holy Virgin', is also painted nearby. In the nave, on the right side is a faded ritual painting of Elisabeth, Ieremia's wife, together with her children. After her husband died, she had a rough life since she never saw her children on the throne for Elisabeth died in a Sultan's harem in Constantinople, but Ieremia and his brother Gheorghe are buried nearby. A stupendous image is 'The Ladder of Virtue', showing angels who assist the righteous to enter Paradise, while sinners (depicted as Turks) fall down to be taken by a grinning hungry demon. The ladder of virtues shows the perilous path that the faithful must tread to reach heaven. Each rung has its corresponding morality. Angels on one side whisper scripture in the ears of heaven-seeking souls, while angels on the other side wage battle against demons who trick weak victims from the true path.

Monks first inhabited Sucevița Monastery in 1582 but during the communist era, only nuns over the age of 50 were allowed to stay. Today it is a convent with the sisters living a simple life in daily prayer, and farming their land. There was ample space around the church to walk and gaze leisurely at the images on the walls. A path set away from the church walls is constructed in slate set in broken patterns like crazy paving. A few trees grow within the fortified enclosure. Restoration work was ongoing but didn't deter from our pleasure, but the museum was closed. Under the main doorway to the church the images were even brighter but a lot of it had been damaged by gratuitous graffiti, damaging any eyes. The stories told by the pictures were portrayed differently than any seen before and images had three-dimensional effects and expressions not at all Byzantine in form, but nevertheless clearly related to it in evolutionary terms.

Inside some of the images were being cleaned and restored but there were numerous others covering other surfaces to admire and try to understand the message portrayed. In the inner sanctum the massive gold covering to the elaborate wooden frames was still to be restored. It is very important of protecting the art for future generations and we wished them all well in their enterprise. The visits to the painted churches had been both an experience and a pleasure and I was so glad that we had made the effort to visit the area.

Roger was getting tired and wanted to take a direct route back to the Marion. So it was south into the foothills of the Obcina Mare with its rounded hills covered in fir trees. The road wound tortuously upwards for a few kilometres before reaching the top of Ciumărna Pass at 1109m to see before us a vast landscape with grasslands dropping away to woods and the Moldaviţa Valley, beyond more forest and the distant mountains of the Obcina Feredeu and Obcina Mestecăniş. It was a magnificent awe-inspiring panoramic view. Following the road down to the valley through many serpentine turns eventually arrived in Vatra Moldoviţei where we turned east at the crossroads to go along the valley southeastward. For most of the way to Vama we followed by the side of a single-track railway sometimes crossing it. At Vama turned eastwards along the valley passing through Frasin to Gura Humorului and then northwards up the valley road to the Marion. Roger was glad to arrive and we had an hour for him to rest and change before dinner, it had been a long but delightful day.

Later in the dining room we found that Roxanne had placed a small decanter on the table of bilberry liqueur, her mother had made, with four small glasses. It was a satisfying drink and had whole bilberries in it. A little later Roxanne brought in a large soup tureen containing a vegetable soup with dumplings made from semolina flour. Next came a bottle of red wine we had ordered for the white wine they had was not cold but unfortunately the red wine turned out to be a demi-sec Merlot.

The soup was an excellent flavor and we were ready for the main course being hungry from the day out. It arrived in stages, first of all a large dish of Macedonian vegetables was brought out then a large dish of baked beaten flat chicken breasts rolled around sausages that were strong tasting like chorizo. These lined the centre of a long dish that had piped delicious mashed potatoes made with butter and cream by Roxanne and was brought in by a smiling proud mother, who cooked most of the meals. When we had finished this very tasty and delectable dish a huge bowl of fresh fruit was brought in. There were pears, beautifully ripe peaches, and both black and green grapes, a fantastic end to a delicious meal.

In conversation with Roxanne we discovered that she was still studying at university, following in the footsteps of her sister, majoring in pharmacy. We hadn't seen her sister for she works late, but I had seen her children in the morning. Currently Roxanne was on holiday so she could help her mother. She said that she had visited friends in London who work at Boots and was surprised about the number of black people in the city and wondered where all the English had disappeared. I assured her that we were a very cosmopolitan multiracial society.

Around Mănăstirea Humorului

September 15th, it was Cicely's birthday and over breakfast she looked at her cards and the presents that Linda and Roger had kindly bought her. She had a beautiful coloured box decorated with butterflies and flowers for holding soap and a notebook with the same decoration on its cover.

Breakfast was a large spread again of an assortment of food, ham and peaches, fried battered cheese, tomatoes, peppers, muesli and cereals, bread, plum jam, butter; enough for everyone.

It was dry outside but the weather had changed to a steel grey pewter sky. After our ample breakfast took a walk to the monastery and both Roger and I strolled through the gate ahead of the girls who had tarried by the stalls, but it turned out that Linda had to pay an entry fee for us later, as the nuns had done a count and noted that we were with her. Inside the church I found that scaffolding had been erected for some restoration work on the frescos and at least three of the four restorers were working there using very fine brushes to apply paint to poor areas. They rested their arms on those padded resting sticks like artists use. As I had seen much of the inside yesterday I went outside to climb the Watch Tower, or perhaps it was the Guard Tower, the one I had sketched anyway.

The first part was easy going via external steps that took you to a room utilizing the whole of the cross section of the tower. The next part of the climb was more difficult via a very narrow stone stair hemmed in by walls that took you to a room with a few glazed windows set into the thick walls of the tower. The last part of the climb to the top was the most difficult of all via a steep stair possible at an angle of 70 degrees even more hemmed in by the walls and with steps of unusual height making it difficult to climb in the dark. I struggled upwards using both the steps and the walls as leverage to finally emerge on the top floor of the tower that was surrounded by wooden balustrades. How soldiers, or ordinary people, climbed those stairs in any emergency I couldn't fathom, nevertheless the view from the top was well worth the effort even though the weather wasn't so good as the previous days for viewing the surroundings. Below the tower at the adjacent farm a group of nuns dressed in black sorted through a large heap of potatoes loading sacks and plastic trays. Nearby was their smart living quarters, which was surrounded by a loggia decked with masses of flowers.

The first part of the way down the tower stressed my knees due to the step height and I was glad to glad to finish the whole descent. I found the others inside of the church being guided by a nun explaining some of the images and the story behind them. I tagged along but didn't hear too well but followed her outside where she explained some more about the frescos on the south wall including the siege of Constantinople. She had already told us that graffiti on some of the walls was done 200 years ago during the Turkish occupation, but one piece of graffiti I noticed was dated from 1885 which was when the land was German and of probably non Orthodox religion.

Nunn's Sorting Potatoes

When we had gathered together again we explored more of the village passing by a number of horse drawn carts carrying hay and admired the elaborate decorative wooden gateways and wooden framed wells. At the cemetery we found a charming garden of flowers set amongst the gravestones. And over in a far field, down in the valley, a group of farmworkers collected potatoes. There were a few butterflies flittering between the flowers, peacocks, painted ladies and whites dominated.

133

A short while later Roger drove us down to Gura Humorului and parked outside the Best Western Hotel. The sky had darkened appreciably and a few spots of rain were falling. Walking westward along the main road keeping to the north side we looked for shops selling wine and shaving cream for I had run out of shaving oil. In a small shop I found some squeeze foam at 10 lei and Linda also found some cotton wool that she wanted. Further along the road we cut left to where there were some stalls one of which was selling CDs of Romanian Folk music, one being played at a high volume. Nearby was an indoor market where we appreciated the vast quantity of good quality fruit and vegetables on display but were mystified by some of the berries that we didn't recognize. Roger spent sometime searching for a leather belt in the stalls and although there were many and not expensive he didn't like the way the belts were constructed. They used staples so he didn't buy one.

Just down from the market at a patisserie bought some cakes for the evening meal to celebrate Cicely's birthday. And while we were there sat down at one of the tables in the café area and ordered coffee choosing some biscuits and cake to have with it while we watched people contending with the rain outside, now falling in stair-rods. When the rain had stopped we left to look at a small supermarket where I managed to find an Asti Spumente and a bottle of dry white wine for the evening; the village was too small to have shops selling champagne. After leaving our purchases in the car, followed a hungry Roger into the Best Western restaurant, as it was lunchtime. Rain was pelting down

134

again and everything looked dismal outside with dejected people raising their umbrellas.

The restaurant was almost empty so had no difficulty in getting a table. I ordered fried chicken livers served in a red wine sauce with French fries as an accompaniment and also with it requested a glass of draught Ursus beer. Roger ordered the same beer and ordered some polenta with bacon too. Linda chose most wisely having a small plate of roast vegetables and Cicely not feeling too hungry ordered only soup and as Linda had a lemon tea to drink. When I had finished my meal I left the others in the restaurant to go and buy a CD from the stall we had seen earlier, as I wanted some authentic music to go with the Romanian DVD I would prepare when at home; in the end I bought two CDs.

The weather showed some improvement, as we drove back up the valley stopping briefly at the Marion to offload our purchases and to give Roxane the cakes and wine for the evening to put in the fridge then drove further up the valley to Poiana Micului. Construction workers were improving both the road and bridges along the way and as the one just outside of Gura Humorului we had to divert from the road down to the streambed and up to the road again for two of the bridges under repair. On the way up the valley a great number of flowering colchicums made a fine autumnal display on grassy banks beside the stream. Eventually the road deteriorated into a stony track so didn't press on through Poiana but returned by the way we had come. A short way out of Poiana we stopped at the roadside to walk over into the fields by the streambed to take photographs of Autumn Crocuses. Unfortunately

135

parts of the field were boggy and at one point my boots sank into the underlying soft mud and had to retreat to higher ground. Back on the road again I spotted a dog that looked starved but it slunk away from me into the trees. Many dogs are seen during any day mostly friendly and well fed. Invariably they go around in pairs and when you see them close up they have scars from injuries sustained in fights. Casual sex takes place often so the dog population either increases, or most probably sustained I would think. Stopping again at another place on the way back to our guesthouse we spotted two white shapes in a field of sheep that didn't move but our conjured images of dead sheep were soon shattered when one shape raised its head and barked. The two dogs moved towards us barking and a third one appeared closer to the fence wagging its tail. They were white sheep dogs and had a wooden bar hanging from a collar in front of them.

Back at the Marion I found my washing had been returned to me as a handsome pile on the settee outside of our room, but there was none for Roger. Later after resting and changing for dinner we went down to the large lounge area. Linda had brought a bag of crisps with her to have with the cool sparkling wine, which Roxanne had brought in; she had been with the children in a neighboring room. Toasting Cicely we nibbled on crisps and sipped our wine discussing what to do for the next days. We agreed that we would spend three nights in Slănic Moldova if the place was OK and another three nights in Bucharest. And the next day we would call in on our way to Slanic at the oldest Monastery in Romania that a friend said would be of interest.

Roxanne came in to say dinner would be ready at seven thirty so moved into the dining room. Soup was served in a large tureen, as previous evenings, carrot and celery based, very tasty and probably used a pork stock as lumps of meat and chopped fresh parsley floated in it. A basket of good bread as well as a carafe of the bilberry liqueur was also brought in. The main course when it arrived was served from a large long plate. Down its centre were slabs of pork loin in a tomato and pepper sauce and down both long sides boiled potatoes that had been tossed in butter and herbs. To have with it was a large bowl of tomato and onion salad. It was all very delicious and enough for second helpings. For desert we had the cakes purchased earlier and throughout the meal drank the dry white wine, which was not too bad. Throughout conversation flowed from experiences with cars and their problems in various holiday places, Sat-Navs and navigation errors, gorge and mountain driving and vertigo experiences and even drunkenness, the evening proved very enjoyable for our last one in Bucovina

Neamt Monastery

Church bells were ringing early and got me up at seven. I could hear a call to the Monastery for the nuns with a banging of their gong. I switched on the TV, the weather forecast indicated the weather would be good. I walked over to the monastery gates where there was a post box to post four cards for Cicely. Down the valley towards Guru Humorului white mist rolled down from the mountains, the sky still cloudy. Many children were going to school, a good sign for a village with so many youngsters. As I walked back to the Marion, the nun's were singing their responses to the priest's prayer. I met Roxanne her hair tumbling down below her shoulders. I don't think she was long out of bed, but good-looking all the same.

At eight all gathered in the dining room for breakfast. Roxanne brought in a large pancake to have with the rest of the food on the table that included a variety of hams and cheeses, two types of cereal muesli and some sugar coated flakes, tomatoes, cucumber, plum jam, and bread. After breakfast we were presented with our bill for 910 lei, which was ridiculously low considering all the food we had had, the wine and the two rooms for three nights so we gave her extra 1000 lei.

Later I took our cases down to load into the car and met Roxanne in the lobby. She wanted me to take some money back but I said it was for her and she seemed pleased. She went on to ask about our further travels in Romania and I also told her what I thought about her country so far. When she was in the UK she knew what a bad reputation it has created in the press through certain elements of Romanian society but I told her that her country didn't do enough marketing to counteract these unfavourable comments. We went on to talk about her degree course and her future ambitions to do a Masters in Toxicology. She went on again about her visit to London being shocked at the time by so many black people that she didn't expect in Europe. I reminded her that Romania had been isolated from the modern cosmopolitan society of Western Europe, which is a magnet for the world's peoples. She would like to join her friend, who works for Boots, getting a job in one of their laboratories too. We talked about the Gypsies and how they were much improved living in houses and working now, and went on about the state of the old communist factories and their legacy. She told me that they were mostly foreign owned and the owners had made no attempt to clear up the pollution they had created. The Romanian government does not have the funds to do the job but they are at least making an effort to change things.

Our farewells said drove south turning eastwards in Guru Humorului. Not far out of town turned right along a country road towards Fălticeni, which is situated on the north south main highway. The landscape was fairly flat farmland with a few workers in the fields and horse drawn carts on the road pulling their harvest loads. Our map was confusing again for we arrived at the main road at Spărtăreşti and later in the day when I bought another map discovered that this was 5km south of Fălticeni. Heading southwards once more along the main road until turning into a country road, at a sign indicating Târgu Neamţ, which passed through a landscape of low hills and farms above the Moldova Valley to the east. Roger was driving too fast down the road but he usually responds well too every situation concerning carts but to his surprise nearly caught out by a flock sheep crossing the road.

Târgu Neamţ had poor road signs in its centre that made it especially difficult to navigate with our poor map to contend with. Our map showed only one cross roads but in fact there turned out to be two. However, we soon realized we were on the wrong road when we turned at the first crossroads for we ended up in a yard with a small lane leading off it to a castle. Turning around we went on to the second crossroads that had a brown sign indicating the direction to the monastery.

The road took us west towards the mountains through scattered woodland and farmland. Eventually, to our right, we saw buildings belonging to the monastery complex down in a valley and shortly afterwards a sign indicated for us to turn down a narrow lane towards the buildings. On arrival there was a large parking space where other cars had been left.

A blurb from a promotional pamphlet is worth recording here to see the dichotomy of views when we had finished the visit. *'Surrounded by old forests, at the foot of the mountains, lies the oldest Orthodox monastery in Moldavia, Neamt Monastery. Founded in the 14th century it is an example of medieval Moldavian architecture. The main church, a jewel of 15th century architecture of the holy establishment 'Ascension of the Lord', was founded by Stefan cel Mare and finished in the year when the Moldavian army won a battle against King John Albert in 1497. Sumptuous and with delicate colour effects, the monastery shows the maturity of the Moldavian style, which matured during Stefan cel Mare's period. The façade of the church is covered with an embellishment characteristic of Stefan cel Mare's time, such as Gothic windows and friezes with enameled disks coloured in green, yellow and brown. The art treasures kept at Neamţ Monastery are proof of the intense artistic and cultural activity, which took place through the centuries. It was here that Gavril Uric showed his talent, and an example is his first known manuscript, dated 1429, that is kept in the Bodleian Library at Oxford. The calligraphers and miniaturists of Stefan cel Mare who worked at this important center made many of the books given to Putna Monastery. In the cells of the monastery, the chronicler Macarie also wrote the chronicle of Petru Rareş's rule, and the Eftimie, the chronicle of Alexandru Lăpuşneanu's rule.'*

Neamţ was different to the Bucovina monasteries; it was much larger and grander in design at least superficially. The monastery was also a home to monks with no nuns in sight, although we discovered later that these did reside in one of the buildings in the outer areas. It has had a history of conflict particularly between the Slavonic peoples and Romanians and originally there were monks from Russia and the Ukraine at the monastery but disputes with the Romanians caused them to leave in the nineteenth century for Bessarabia.

After parking the car near to a domed building outside of the walled complex, which was situated in attractive parkland with many trees. Across from us at the entrance to the walled enclosure a monk sat at a table taking money from visitors. However, we all wanted to visit the toilets, which were situated just over from us, they turned out to be quite filthy and by the time we were ready to enter the complex no one was collecting money, so we walked in through a tower archway gate that had frescos of poor quality covering it.

All Seeing Eye Gateway Neamt Monastery

Inside the walls it was almost a square ground plan with continuous two storey rooms topped with sloping roofs. To one side stood two churches one of which had a small tower. On the right hand side were the monks' quarters and on the grass a few monks were engaged in cleaning and preparing a huge heap of carrots. I thought that they might be making a large quantity of carrot soup for the seventy monks who live there but Roger thought that they would be making some preparation for an alcoholic beverage. Later we learnt from a monk that it was indeed for soup, at least not admitting it was alcohol.

In the first church we expected to see some fine frescos, but the inside was dark and depressing with grimy walls. It was the same in all three rooms the last having an altar screen. The lightest room was the first we had entered but it was much too gloomy for good photography. I was sure that there must be some good frescoes there, but they were just not clean enough, or lit well enough to appreciate them. The silver work was badly tarnished and all the paintings were in a need of a good clean, as was the wooden screen. It just needed some tender loving care and the monks obviously didn't give it. Disappointed we moved on to the next church that had brighter mosaic figures on the outside but again the former glorious frescoes were covered in centuries of grime and dirt. Moreover, it looked as if at some time in the past someone with no art experience had attempted to clean them and destroyed the images for they were patched with protective coverings. We left again disappointed from what might have been a treasure if only we could have seen it. Even the frescos in the dome were covered in grunge.

Glad to be outside again in the fresh air and sunshine I walked over to the group of monks cleaning and preparing their carrots. One sat by a bucket of water

144

scrubbing carrots clean after taking them from a sack, he then passed them on to another monk who shredded them in a large commercial shredder while three other monks stood around looking on. They definitely were going to make a lot of soup.

I noticed a sign to the museum by the gateway and walked over to it climbing steps to an entrance lobby and on through to the museum. On the wall hung paintings of no particular merit, but further stairs led me into a large room with more pictures and heavy wooden cases housing church relics and bits of archeology probably found around the site. They didn't look like proper archeological finds for there was no information about them. The pictures were of unknown places and some old photographs of the monastery. There was nothing too exciting, like the casket with a cloth covering I had seen in the church, supposedly of a body exposing part of a rib bone. The only exception was a cabinet housing the crown of Stefan cel Mara, Prince of Moldavia 1457 to 1504. In another room there were old printing presses and examples of pamphlets and books. Some were old bibles, others scientific works judging by the illustrations of blood vessels and some drawings of moon and planetary motions. The place was well below par for normal tourist curiosity but I had read that the library at the monastery contains 18,000 rare books.

I followed the others outside of the main gate over to the dome-like building, the Baptistery, that Roger told me had maps for sale. On entering it the first impressions were of a disorderly arrangement of books in stacks around the outer walls and on tables. Bright,

145

near to garish, modern inferior frescos, covered the inside of the dome and a large stone dish stood beneath the centre, probably originally a font. A plump happy smiling monk presided over the place. I found a useful map book at 1:500,000 rather than the 1:1,000,000 and bought it.

We drove off going back the same way as we had come in from Târgu Neamț, and on nearing the town saw the massive ruined walls of the old castle on its rocky crag surrounded by woods. Neamț Citadel (Romanian: Cetatea Neamț or Cetatea Neamțului) is a Moldavian medieval fortress built in the 14th century, during Petru the First's reign, and was expanded during the 15th century. The citadel played a key role in Stephen III of Moldavia's defense system, along with Suceava, Hotin, Soroca, Orhei, Tighina, Chilia and Cetatea Albă.

On reaching the country road again we turned right and headed south towards Piatra Neamț passing through farmland high above the plain to the east. Just before Piatra Neamț the road turned in a large loop around a hill to descend rapidly into the town. The area around Piatra Neamț is one of the oldest inhabited areas in Romania with traces of human civilization dating back to Paleolithic times, about 100,000 years BC. Settlements from the Cucuteni culture have been found and excavated. Finds have shown that their development in the area lasted approximately from 3600-2600 BC. Archaeological digs have unearthed important Aeneolithic (transition between Neolithic and Bronze Age when some copper was used) artifacts displayed in museums and archaeologists have also discovered other objects dating back to the Neolithic

Period and the Bronze Age. Excavations just outside of the town have also revealed ruins of a large Dacian city, Petrodava, mentioned by the Greek geographer Ptolemy in the 2nd century. The whole compound had its heyday between the first century BC and the first century AD. A complex of strongholds has shown it to be a powerful political and military centre. The settlement was known in the 15th century as Piatra lui Craciun, or Camena, when it was a market town.

Piatra Neamț was not easy to navigate through even with the new map, for on the town map I had confused a stream Pr Cuejdiut with the Bistrița River and told Roger to turn left at it going in the wrong direction however I soon realized my mistake and got back on track by following signs to Bacău. Just out of town Roger turned off the dual carriageway along a dusty stony lane between domestic houses parking by a house with bunches of black grapes hanging down from vines in the garden. At breakfast the girls had made sandwiches and it was these we were stopping to eat. Curious children were coming out of school probably going home for lunch. An old woman wearing a headscarf typical of the region came out as well to inspect us and crossed the road to enter another house. Occasional cars traveling down the road kicked up a lot of dust so I moved back inside the car to eat my sandwich.

Later we drove on to Slanic Moldova.

Slănic Moldova

Roger was driving fast again along the road to Bacău; it was long and tedious driving into the sun. Once we were within the confines of the large town navigation became difficult. The town is the main industrial centre of Moldavia and provides the largest contribution to the country's GDP. In fact Bacău's hey day began in the twentieth century when oil was discovered nearby and became under communist rule one of the most industrialized regions in Romania. There are two large oil refineries at Oneşti and Dărmăneşti.

The road signs in the town left much to be desired and were not always consistent in giving the places that had been shown before, for instance there was a sign to Slănic Moldova just after entering the town, but then not given again for some time; I knew though that we must keep west of the river. I tended to follow the signs to Bucharest for again we had to get onto Route 2 from the north and had only to drive along it for a very short distance. Although I told Roger to keep to the inside lane he was impatient and left the lane to pass other vehicles consequently missing our turning which was clearly labelled. It wasn't surprising that Roger got irritated since he had been driving for a long time into the sun. He thought, quite rightly, I should have picked out the Braşov sign that was the largest town more or less in the direction we wanted. Taking the responsibility for navigating he turned right off the Bucharest road and followed a van taking us through a network of narrow town roads but eventually we emerged on the right road out of town, Roger is always good following his instincts.

Relaxed again after the hiatus of Bacău we followed the route to Onesti towards the mountains, the Munţii Vrancei. At Oneşti, that is renowned for its petrochemical industry, we skirted most of the town's industrial plants to drive westward towards Tărgu Ocna that is situated on the left bank of the Trotuş River, an tributary of the Siret River. Târgu Ocna is built among the Carpathian Mountains on bare hills formed of rock salt, in fact the English translation of Ocna is salt mine. The main industry is salt production and is the largest provider in Moldavia. Other industries include wood processing, coal mining, steel producing, and petroleum-based industries.

Leaving Tărgu Ocna we turned left along a heavily wooded valley into the hills and on towards Slănic Moldova only a few kilometres away. We passed by a poor looking village with a few oil derricks seen here and there. The country road took us on up the valley passing by a National park to emerge into a strange collection of buildings; it was the place we were to stay. It was a mixture of faded Belle Époque buildings and communist concrete monstrosities but the whole place had an air of decay about; it wasn't at all what I had expected. Roger drove through the resort for us to look

150

for suitable hotels. Perhaps there were good ones but as it turned out we didn't have a chance to find out.

According to tourist literature Slănic-Moldova is a well-known and very beautiful Romanian spa resort situated on the eastern slope of the Eastern Carpathians, in the foothills of Nemira massifs. Forests of beeches and fir trees surround its location, at an elevation of 530 m, in a valley of the Slănic beck, a tributary of Trotuş River. The descriptions of the place did not tie in with our first impressions, which were 'why are we here?' but in former times and still probably by Romanians, or Moldavians, it is a resort appreciated for its unique variety of mineral springs in terms of their composition, concentration and complexity of both chemical and therapeutic effects. It was first discovered for its spa potential and exploited at the beginning of the nineteenth century and by 1887 became a well known Spa Town. Our guidebook informed us that the resort has many hotels and villas, a sanatorium complex and various facilities and opportunities for recreation and amusement, concert halls, gaming halls, sports grounds, bowling alley, and disco. And goes on to describe the environment as a wild and fascinating landscape that offers the opportunity of short walks in the shady, quiet, narrow valley.

Typical of Roger he turned up one of the broken potholed roads that led to a communist looking tower block that was dilapidated, looking the worse for wear. I accompanied Roger into the large lobby where a cheery enough man said they had rooms for 50 to 70 lei per night but only for two nights as a party of 200 was arriving on Sunday. We stepped back out onto rough

151

crumbling overgrown debris where a couple of old people sat on a concrete block staring at us. Back in the car we found out that the girls didn't like the place and I agreed with them. Going back the way we had come and driving on through once more we came to the bottom of a stair that led to what looked like a fine 5-star boutique hotel. I climbed up the many steep crumbling, often dangerous, neglected steps to a front door that had a sign stating 'Private Members Club'. Carefully I backtracked down the steps to the car and Roger drove off once more. There seemed to be nothing around except for not very attractive 2-star hotels and a restaurant or two. But further up the road at the top end of the town we saw a promising looking place, The Coroana, a 4-star hotel. It had four storeys the last being in the sloping roof moreover it was freshly painted. We parked up a rough stony lane between the hotel and what looked to be one of the old communist tower buildings that was being renovated or rebuilt in places. It looked awful and high steel fencing surrounded a space at the bottom end by the main road. We learned later that the renovation work had been on going for ten years because the owners had run out of money a few times. The part surrounded by the fence was eventually planned to be a swimming pool and the only workmen we saw were working on painting the main building.

I went up the steps to the Coroana and through the door into reception. A jolly well-built man sat at a desk in reception and by his side a younger man stood erect in a hotel uniform. He informed me that they had two double rooms for three nights and at a price of 50 euros. I said to him that my wife and friend should look at the rooms. Returning to the car the girls said that they would look but make no commitment because they wanted to view other hotels.

The young man in uniform took us up the stairs to show us the rooms on the second floor. The rooms looked to be of good size and had en-suite facilities but as we left one of the rooms we spotted Roger scampering up the stairs to the next floor following a largish woman. We were quite surprised since he promised to stay in the car. Following them up to the third floor we were shown two rooms that looked out onto the old communist building, or what was to be the swimming pool. They were pleasant enough with good-looking en-suite facilities but as with the entire hotel the décor was a little over the top faux Belle Époque. Madame hovered near to us saying 'Very Good, Very Good'. She also told us that the room opposite contained a Jacuzzi that we could use and looking in it we saw some kind of tent arrangement too that looked like a portable Turkish bath, but I didn't think Linda was too keen on this contraption.

Roger didn't like the room at the front and wanted to see one at the side. It was smaller but had a larger wardrobe. Of the two rooms we liked 301 at the front. We all went down stairs but Roger shook hands with the man on reception saying we would take the rooms, much to the annoyance of the girls. The rooms were 50 euro or 200 lei per night including breakfast. He said that there was no hotel elevator but that he would get one of the boys to take our bags up and he would also move his car so that Roger could park in his place by the fence.

When we went up to our rooms again after the bags had been carried up we discovered that both rooms had only one bedside light working, but you couldn't really call it a bedside light for it was half way up the wall. However, the worst for Roger was the shower for it had no fittings to hold the nozzle so he was all for leaving. We calmed him down and sat him on the settee outside of the rooms and eventually he agreed to stay. Rather than unpacking our bags we went down to the terrace to have a drink but called in at reception to tell them about the lights and to get more pillows, he said he would attend to it. He also went on to tell us about the attractions of the area, a walk up the stream to see the various water sources that he advised us not to drink, also a local salt mine to visit and a monastery that was also good to see.

Sitting out on the terrace that overlooked part of the fencing surrounding the hotel being restored we looked at the painters at work on the wall of the tower block. Three of them launched themselves over the side of the roof on ropes dangling down the wall and sat on wooden planks like a swing. Linda thought that the activity was a little precarious but they did have a safety rope and harness. After finishing our welcome beers we left to walk down through the town. It was a bizarre resort with many things requiring maintenance; roads were in a shambolic state but the park area that we walked through had elements of its former grandeur, even though it too was neglected. There was a weird atmosphere; a few, mostly old people, sat on park benches with vacant staring eyes. Linda said it was like being on the stage set of 'The Prisoner', waiting for something to happen. One or two of the buildings looked much better though and if they were all brought up to that standard then the place would come alive. Roger and I went into one of hotels leaving the girls to walk down the road to some stalls. It was much plusher than the one we had booked into and of the same price moreover it had more facilities. Roger said, 'Don't tell Linda'. In the end we didn't walk far and returned to the Coroana a little depressed with the ambiance.

Dinner in the hotel restaurant that evening was on the top floor and turned out to be a miserable affair for all except for me. I had a starter of mushroom with Gorgonzola cheese followed by a main course of carp cutlet served with tomato salad and frites, both courses I enjoyed, conversely though the dessert was a bit too much. I had ordered the Papanasi with no cream but it arrived on a large plate, two large donuts plastered with sour cherry jam. I ate one of them and left the rest. The others sat with scorn on their faces around a table full of food debris, dried meat, messed up fish and piles of brown potatoes and mushrooms. Yet Roger did finish off with a Finneti, which is like a hazelnut spread on a Pancake, but Cicely hardly ate anything at all and wanted a good glass of liqueur to compensate, unfortunately they didn't have one to her liking.

The next day after a good night's sleep we woke to a fine sunny morning. Later we climbed the stairs to have breakfast in the restaurant where a number of people were already eating. Taking a table by a window we fetched various things from the buffet to eat. There was quite a choice to select from with two types of cereal including muesli, various cooked things in trays such as various sausages, fried egg, omelet, as well as salads, tomato, peppers, cheese and bread and jam. The coffee though was inferior being from an urn.

After breakfast we walked up the wooded valley following Slănic beck via a footpath we had seen on a map displayed on a board by the sources where people filled up water containers. The map had showed four stopping points to take the waters; we sensibly declined, as the chemical stains on the rock over which they flowed were a colourful warning. As we moved higher up the valley, mostly in the shade of trees, the path diverged away from the stream becoming a wider dirt track. Continuing onwards up hill emerged eventually from shade into full sunshine, the many wild flowers in bloom added to the pleasant surroundings. During the walk observed about five different species of butterfly, including a fritillary with triangular wing formation, and an unknown reddish brown one and Cicely saw a copper too. We even saw someone drilling for oil in the streambed, judging from machinery mounted on a lorry that was parked beside the track. About half a mile further on passed through the hamlet of Baile Slănic and it was not long afterwards a cart pulled by two horses came towards us. It was piled high with bedding covering cut tree trunks. Five lads were on board and passed us by trotting at speed.

I walked back down the hill with Linda, Roger was with Cicely not too far behind searching out butterflies. Back at the resort we walked down through the town to a Pizza restaurant situated at the end of the park area and elevated above the main road. It was a large restaurant with people already eating. The sides were open to the elements and had flowers in boxes suspended on walls below. We ordered pizzas with a vinegar dressed beetroot and pepper salad, plus beers all round.

After lunch Roger drove us down the valley to visit the salt mine in the small town of Tărgu Ocna. Got tickets at an office in the grounds of a number of industrial looking buildings. A bus that was to take us down into the mine was located in a lower area accessed by steps. Found the minibus almost full but the girls managed to get seats and Roger too, but I had to stand near to the front. When all was ready the driver got in and drove off to enter a tunnel bored into the hillside above the complex. It had dressed stone surrounds and a sign situated over the tunnel arch stating 'Mina Trotus'.

The trip down into the mine was exciting driving over a bumpy road surface mostly in a downward spiral, the driver keeping steering on full lock. I was glad to get out of the bus when it arrived at last within a vast open underground cavern. When everyone had disembarked we were ushered through a high curtained wall. The temperature was much lower than on the surface, around ten degrees, so I put on my fleece, as did the others. Beyond the curtain entered a large spacious place with square cross-sectioned chambers off it rising to a height of a three-storey house. The mine workings were cut out in a grid with equal column dimensions to those of the hollow chambers. St Varvara Church was located in the first chamber. It had brightly coloured icons including one that looked like St George killing a dragon, but in the shape of an octopus. Left to our own

157

devices, we looked around other chambers but there wasn't much to see. In one there was a museum with not enough of the labels in English to fathom out what it was all about, in another a shop sold masks and painted icons, in others were a five aside football pitch, a basketball court and a kiddies play area. In another part of the salt mine was a pumped waterfall with a pond below in which yellow plastic ducks bobbed around. And strangely in another area coloured plaster Gnomes were positioned incongruously. My thoughts went straight to John Major our prime minister in the 90's, his brother was famous for selling them, and perhaps he ventured into Romanian territory.

According to the official literature the church built inside a salt dome on level nine was the first underground Orthodox Church in Europe. It is dedicated to St.Varvara, because she is known as the miners' protector. It was built during 1992 on the initiative of the mine employees. At the altar is a set of twenty-four icons, the far left and far right ones representing St. Varvara and St. Parascheva, the patron saint of Moldavia. The bishop's throne and the fixtures are all carved in salt sculpted by miners then varnished with some special substance to make them look like wood. The Salt Museum was set up inside the salt mine to show the origin and evolution of salt exploitation. It displays some historical, archeological and other sorts of documents and photographs together with collections of mineral samples.

We took a full-length bus back to the surface that was much more comfortable and warm too. On the drive back up to the Coroana we passed by people in fields collecting hay into piles as well spying a few rusty oilrigs that didn't seem to be operational. At the hotel Roger wanted to rest, so I fetched my sketchbook and went down through the park to draw the casino building that had an elaborate architecture. I sat in the sunshine on one of the park benches hoping for peace and quiet.

Casino at Slănic-Moldova

I found sketching difficult for two main reasons the first being the complex shape and peculiar perspective the second people were inquisitive. There were many more people out and about as it was a weekend and on finishing wasn't too pleased with my effort and thought that I must get an eraser.

Later I bumped into Cicely who had been taking photographs so we went back to the hotel together. In our room I thought that the towels had been changed but found they hadn't and bizarrely wet towels had been removed from the bathroom and rolled up and placed by our bed. There are many features of the hotel that are hard to fathom. This morning Linda showed me the toilet just below the top floor, off the stairs, where the door height is only four foot, perhaps built for children or midgets. The other that is much more dangerous is an uneven drop of steps on the stairs some being quite high, particularly the first one down from floor three, which if you don't watch out you can jar your knee. And the stairs to the top floor are made of wood not of marble as the other stairs. This is opposite to the image the hotel wants to give of fake Belle Époque.

Earlier we had said that we would not risk the hotel restaurant again and that we would find a restaurant in town. It was seven thirty when we walked down Str Vasile Alecsandri the highest road in town down from our hotel. Roger and I had discovered it in the morning at the Vila Teleconstrucția hotel. It was supposed to be the best restaurant in town according to the label on the outside. On arrival a charming young woman showed us to a table in a fine dining room near to a large circular table that had been set out for a group of children. She said that our meal would be delayed a little, but at the same time brought us some olives, bread and two carafes of Moldavian wine, one white and one red. While we waited a group of thirty children of ages probably ranging from five to eleven came in with two teachers. They were quiet and orderly and sat down waiting for their meal to arrive of meat in gravy

160

with polenta. A short prayer was said and their meal served. They ate silently with no disturbance to the rest of the customers in the dining room. We learnt from Elena when she came to take our orders that the children were not from an orphanage, as we first thought, but from poor farm worker's families. One or two of the children looked thin but most seemed to be happy. They had been taken on visits during the day and were staying somewhere nearby. We found out that 'World Vision', a Christian charity from the USA, supported the meal and both Roger and I decided to give the teachers 200 lei each to buy the children ice creams for they would only have a one course meal. We gave the money to Elena for her to take to the teachers. They came over to thank us warmly but could speak no English; Elena though translated for us what they said. Elena had learnt to speak English by first reading comic books then in school up to eighth grade.

Our first course arrived. It was cheese croquettes served with a tomato salad. For the main course I had the Moldavian Stew that Elena recommended. It had in it small pieces of succulent pork, some sausage and pieces of bacon and was served with polenta. It also had a poached egg on top with a scattered of sharp cheese, a delicious dish. Linda had chicken livers cooked in red wine and served with green beans and sauté potatoes, Cicely had a filet of perch baked in an almond crust topped with browned flaked almonds and served with a mixture of vegetables and Roger had the same starter as me plus some pork stew served with a Greek salad. During the meal a second sitting of children arrived looking to be from secondary schools. Again they were well behaved and caused little disturbance in the room. Unfortunately we didn't know when we gave the money that there would be sixty of them, but perhaps they would just buy ice creams for the young ones

Finally we indulged in dessert. I had two types of ice cream, Cicely two Fineti pancakes, and Roger a macaroni cheese. Finally Elena came with our bill and we discovered that although she was Moldavian she wasn't of Slavic decent, but Romanian. After paying both Elena and a man, we thought to be the manager we had seen earlier on arrival, came out with us and wished us well for the rest of our holiday; although our tip had been good it wasn't too large but I think that they appreciated what we had done for the children for we thought that the hotel had done a lot too. Pleased with our meal we said that we would return tomorrow.

A starry sky greeted us outside, the temperature still warm and pleasant. Unfortunately illumination from the street lights blocked out most of the stars in the sky, which I suspected would be magnificent here with such clear air. It was ten thirty, as we walked back up the empty silent street happy after a wonderful meal, but on arrival at our hotel found it all in darkness. In the jocular mood we were in I said that they had locked us out but soon discovered they had. I pressed the bell several times but nothing happened. Cicely gave Roger a torch for I had found a side door that was open off the terrace inside though found only the boiler room with no other door within. Linda intelligently used her mobile to phone the hotel. The Gauleiter, the wife of the manager, who had tried to persuade us to take the rooms on arrival and who sits at breakfast unsmiling

162

and officious, answered Linda and said she would be down shortly. After a minute the lights came on and the door opened. There stood Madame in all her glory dressed in a nightgown. Linda was annoyed and set about her but the Gauleiter shrugged it off in her usual fashion, "Hotel Full", she said. And that was all, no apology. Roger said that he would ask for a key in the morning.

Woke early to another fine day with a clear blue sky, the sun yet to illuminate the valley. According to the TV the weather would remain good for the next two days at least. Met with Linda and Roger at breakfast sitting in our usual place by the window. There were more people in that yesterday and the cook behind the bar looked sternly at me, as I helped myself to most of the muesli in the container that she had to fill up again. Later I indulged in an omelet, but it tasted funny, Cicely said that it was probably a dirty pan it was cooked in. Judging from the cook's repertoire I thought it could be anything from fish to pork, but most probably smoky bacon. It's funny she'd fill a whole container with a mixture of sausage, omelets and bacon. I finished with a piece of marbled cake and had some fresh slices of apple from Linda; the cook kept her eye on me the whole time.

When the Gauleiter came in to the restaurant she just nodded to us; we are now persona non grata. The weather girl on the TV wears a white micro mini and very high heel shoes and struts prancing like a new born foal showing off her long legs. A hyperactive little boy with a cap gets away from his mother yet again and rattled some keys he had near to the screen. When his

163

cap came off it exposed his shaven head. As we left the restaurant he came with us to the door where the stairs fall away steeply. I put my arm out to stop him falling down the stairs but his mother was soon there after accelerating fast across the floor in a frantic movement with fear in her eyes. She smiled her thanks at me and carried off the struggling lad back to her table for the umpteenth time.

We asked the manager in reception about last night. He apologized saying it wouldn't happen again. His explanation was that the young man on duty had some illness and had to leave the desk so locked up. I didn't believe him.

Roger drove us up the road past the cascade and on to a rough road that wound its way up the mountain through dense woods twisting and turning. In places the road looked as if at one time it had been cobbled and occasional old concrete edges were seen through the undergrowth. The road was full of potholes and just after another sharp bend became like a rough streambed with boulders and deep ruts. Even Roger thought this to be too difficult to attempt drive up with our hire car so backed up to park off the road on a flat grassy area.

We continued walking on up the hill hoping to emerge from the densely packed conifer trees to view the surrounding landscape. In places we could detect the former pavé road surface, but poor maintenance and bad weather had probably destroyed the road that was further aggravated by heavy forestry cart traffic, or perhaps even lorries. Remains of an old stonewall and concrete fixtures indicated long forgotten barriers; at one time it must have been a good road. Glimpses of sunbeams through the trees lit up a ridge on the hill, but we never did clear the trees and the laborious upward walk became so boring we turned around to walk back to the car. Bird noise was missing, the environment silent and still.

Roger drove us back to the hotel for a ten-minute break before driving us down to the Vila Teleconstrucţia where we had dinner the previous evening. Elena greeted us and said for us to go into the dining room and to sit at one of the tables. We said that we wanted to eat there in the evening and she gave us the menu to look at. She was smartly dressed in a decorative white cotton blouse designed with sown over panels in both chevron and vertical stripes. It also had a round neck and short sleeves in its highly fashionable look. She also had on a black wrap around skirt laced up on the left side showing a bare leg to the thigh and wore dangly gold earrings and black high heel shoes that finished off the whole effect. Her hair was pulled back into a plated single pigtail that fell to her waist. She said that I could take a photograph and smiled at me with pleasure.

I chose the perch in wine sauce with green beans. Cicely chose a chicken dish with honey and in discussion with Elena found out that there would be a side dish of special wild mushrooms from the woods that were in season but we could also have it as a starter. Roger ordered some pork dish and Linda baked perch with vegetables. After she had taken our orders for the main course she said to follow her, as she would show us the indoor swimming pool. It was large and Linda said she

165

would like to try it out, Elena said we were all welcome to do so. We then thanked her saying we would be there at seven thirty in the evening.

It was hot outside as Roger drove down towards Tărgu Ocna hoping to find the road to the monastery. I had looked at the map but found none marked but after entering the small village of Cerdac a brown road sign indicated the Monastery of Stefan cel Mare to our right. It was a narrow tarmacked road that soon deteriorated into a stony track that ascended the hillside behind the village. The state of the track worsened, as we rose higher with the Monastery still 6km away. We drove on through areas of birch trees and open land exposing us to a panoramic landscape of valley and mountains. The view was exceptional back up the valley towards Slanic where distant mountain peaks changed from blue to light grey and faded into the sky. After passing a hill farm we saw other vehicles coming down the mountain towards us, they were mainly 4X4's and shortly afterwards saw the monastery on a distant ridge partially obscured by trees. The road looped around the hillside until it came to a fork. I thought we should drive straight on up towards the satellite repeater station we saw up above us but Linda disagreed and said to take the left fork but after going only 100m Roger stopped thinking that the road wasn't right because it looked to be curving around the hillside to drop back down into the valley.

I recced where the road was going by climbing up a bank to a plateau area where there were remains of a capped off oilrig, but to my right further up the hill I could see the tops of the monastery building complex.

166

My original route at the fork was right and went back to Roger to tell him but he wasn't satisfied. I went out a second time to go beyond the plateau area and went further along the road. I saw my first oil derrick close up and another further along the road that had a working donkey pump. The road continued on past this with no signs of a road turning up the hill to the right and it looked as if the road would eventually descend into the valley far below. I walked back to the car where the others were gathered looking at the surroundings.

Roger drove back to the fork where another car was on its way down. We drove on up to the monastery and parked the car outside near to a gateway. The monastery looked newly built and well looked after. A brown horse was in a fenced off paddock near to the gate rubbing its head on a wooden post rail. Beyond it a tremendous view of the wooded valley and mountain range.

The white walled gateway had three small towers on top with a witch's hat finish in red-brown tiles. I followed Roger through the arched entrance into the stone walled enclosure. A stone slab pathway led up a rise flanked by low stone walls topped at intervals with stone pillars connected by three wooded rails and bordered on the other side with flowering roses and very short cypress trees.

Roger mounted marble steps up to a small white walled church to go inside while I looked around outside. The church had white rendered walls over a bare stone base and on its overhanging tiled roof was a tower built in two tiers and finished off with a witch's hat. Other

167

buildings too were contained within the walls of the complex and a large one beyond the church looked like living quarters with many flowers within its surrounding garden. It gave a good feeling and especially on a day like we had with an intense blue sky with sunshine reflecting off the white surfaces.

The Monastery was founded in 1999 by Vasile Gavrila and in 2003 construction of the church started. On the Feast of Saint Stephen in 2006 the Great Slănic Monastery was completed and the church consecrated.

I followed Roger up the steps to the church noticing three new frescos painted in the old style above the doorway. Inside there were three rooms as usual with all walls covered in brightly coloured frescos in traditional Byzantine style similar to previous churches we had been to, in addition to this was the portrayal of two abbots; there was also an icon of Stefan cel Mare in silver. The next room I entered was under the tower with a ceiling octagon portraying Christ Pantokrator. Roger had been investigating what was behind the screen and I turned on instinct to see standing behind me a young bearded monk without a hat his long flowing hair tied back in a ponytail. He didn't speak any English so I continued taking photographs of the images not wanting to stop and then moved back towards the entrance followed by the monk. St Stephan's emblem was over the doorway into room two; I gave the monk 10 lei, which he seemed pleased with.

Having seen enough we went back outside into the sunshine followed by the monk. Roger tried to converse with him asking if there was another way down to the valley. He had some words of English but indicated that the quickest way down was past the oil derricks. It was only 3km but the first 1km was very rough and difficult to drive along. We expressed our thanks to the monk and he left for his quarters as we took the path back to the gate and the car.

Sensibly Roger decided to drive back down the way we had come up. It was much easier going down and were soon at the Slănic road where we turned left to drive back to the hotel. There were many more tourists around than before and the place was quite crowded. Roger had to find a place elsewhere to park the car.

Band Stand Slănic-Moldova

We walked down to the pizza restaurant we had used for lunch yesterday, as our hotel didn't do lunches in the bar area. The place was busy but we found a table and ordered two pizzas, a cabbage salad, three beers and a lemon tea for Cicely. After lunch Roger went back to the hotel to rest and read his book, while Linda and Cicely said they wanted to do some shopping at the supermarket so I took my backpack with my sketchbook and pencils to sit on a bench on the bankside overlooking a domed grandstand. I found it a little hot sitting in the full sun but was loth to leave. The density of people going past me was much less than yesterday and didn't bother me. My art isn't up to much and I felt that I was getting worse sketching with my long distant glasses it just doesn't work. Cicely came by to visit and asked me when I was going back to the hotel, I said about five. Linda apparently had gone back to the hotel after shopping but we discovered later that she had gone swimming in the pool at Elena's place. The time went on and my sketching didn't improve so I went back up towards the hotel and discovered on the way Cicely photographing butterflies in a meadow and went back to the hotel together.

Back in our room we found that the bedding had been changed and arranged in their peculiar fashion, but it didn't take us long to change it to how we liked it, such a strange hotel. I then showered and changed for dinner.

It was a warm evening when later we walked down to the Vila Teleconstrucţia where Elena was waiting for us smiling happily in her greeting before showing us to our table. I ordered a starter of pickled fungus and some potato wedges to go with my perch in wine sauce with green beans. I also ordered the Papanasi for dessert made with a cottage cheese filling. With our starters Elena brought us a small carafe of bilberry liqueur with four small glasses. The starters included some mashed cooked vegetables like a ratatouille mix. In conversation I asked Elena whether she could recommend any hotels in Bucharest, hearing this her partner began looking on the Web from his laptop.

The meal was excellent and during it Elena's partner looked through many hotel options and called Roger over a few times to look at them and get his advice. He eventually homed in on one called Hotel Unique and before dessert called us both over to look at it. We agreed to go ahead with the booking and booked it on line and were given a print out. They both had been extremely helpful to us so we tipped them well, as the meal and the service had been excellent too. Before leaving Elena and her partner wished us well and presented us with two bottles of local wine. Elena kissed us and her partner shook our hands gratefully then waved goodbye from the top of the steps, as we walked back up to our hotel. Along the way we met the two young men from the hotel who had previously helped us out. It was their evening off and they looked like they we dressed to kill and off to a dance at the Casino disco where we had seen many girls entering on our way to dinner.

The manager was on duty when we got back and he wished us goodnight. On our landing area a young couple sat on a settee drinking wine. Their baby we had seen them with earlier was asleep on their balcony. They were from Bucharest and had just started their holiday finding the hotel through the Web. They thought Slănic strange too but were only staying for a couple of days then they would head north.

Bucharest

It was another fine sunny morning as we went up to breakfast. A different chef was on duty, a male one who was much more pleasant and prepared scrambled eggs for us. After breakfast we paid our bill at reception, 714 lei for three nights and one diner and said goodbyes to the maid before leaving. The manager gave us a hotel card when we said goodbye to him perhaps hoping we would recommend his hotel to others.

It was nine twenty when Roger drove off down the secluded valley and eventually on through Onesti to the wide Siret Valley reaching National Highway, E85, at Adjud. This city is situated on a plain and is surrounded by hills up to a height of 400 meters at the foot of the southern Carpathians. The average altitude of the town is 100 m above sea level and the surrounding land very favorable for agriculture fed by both the Trotuş and Siret rivers. We were now in the county of Vrancea.

Legend has it that the name Vrancea is derived from Baba Vrancioaia, mother of seven brave and handsome men, which she sent to fight with the Moldavian Voivode (War Leader and Leader in a Province), Steven the Great, to help him in one of the wars against the

Turks. Later as a reward for their bravery shown in battle Steven gave them seven mountains to reign over creating a county to be named Vrancea. It became known as the County of Wines and Vineyards and is situated just outside the Carpathian Crescent at the crossroads of three historical regions: Moldova, Muntenia and Transylvania. It is blessed with good fertility and climate and produces many good wines.

We headed south across the seemingly ever expanding plain passing by numerous vineyards and maize fields. I thought if modern agricultural techniques were introduced here then the region could become the 'bread basket' of Europe bringing to Romania an economic richness they deserve. Clouds began to form, as we pushed south to Buzau. On reaching this large town we stopped just off the bypass to refuel and have a coffee and snack. I bought two pastries one filled with bilberries and the other with a sharp cheese plus a double-espresso. Cicely and Roger bought lemon tea but Linda had a coffee too but said it was all froth and no substance. Cicely always tempted by chocolate bought a Ritter bar of hazelnut and dark chocolate.

Moving on once more we drove fast along an elevated section of the highway above the plain heading for Bucharest. The two-lane highway had no central barrier and the width of the lanes was not the same, the narrower lane being on the inside. It was quite dangerous in places particularly in villages when vehicles emerged from side streets. Recently the government has enacted legislation banning horses and carts on all main roads in an effort to reduce the number of road accidents for Romania has the highest recorded number of fatal car accidents in Europe. But changes like this cannot be taken without due consideration to farming communities and their livelihood. In their economic situation people currently depend upon horses and horse-drawn carts and use them in many ways, such as for travel, to plough fields, for gathering in their harvest and to carry items to sell at market. The ban has consequently provoked an outcry especially since they caused only 10% of all accidents in the country. But action is definitely needed as one person dies in every three car crashes in Romania in comparison to the rest of the EU when there's a victim for every 40 accidents. Some experts believe the large number of fatal car accidents is a result of a drivers' inability to drive defensively, the bad roads, and the poor highways.

When we reached the village of Afumati at a right-angled bend to our left Roger drove straight on down a village road, for he wanted his lunch. We had made sandwiches at breakfast and also had some biscuits and fruit with us.

Refreshed from the break Roger drove off fast on the last leg to Bucharest. In a few kilometers we turned right onto the ring road signposted Ploiești. The road was more like a motorway with two lanes and a central reservation. I looked out for the Route 1 ramp off it, the road we wanted was the one we had taken at the start of our travels but from the airport that was to the north of us. It turned out to be the third exit but to make our turn we had to pass under a flyover and turn left across the traffic flow to go up the ramp to a highway densely

175

packed with traffic.

I had a sheet with landmark directions, noted the night before. I gave Roger instructions aiming for Piaţa Romana, via Piaţa Presei Libere, the Arcul de Triumf, and Piaţa Victoriei that I had picked up off a town map in the Lonely Planet Guide. The journey at first was straightforward. I had told the girls about the landmarks and we ticked them off as we passed them by, including the massive arch. The tree-lined road we were driving along had four lanes all densely packed with vehicles. When we had passed through Piaţa Victoriei I told Roger to keep to the inside lane but seeing his chances to pass traffic he changed lanes and that was our downfall. At Piaţa Romana the outside lanes carried on through the square leaving the inside lanes for traffic to rotate around the square just what we should have done. But Roger always unfazed drove straight down Bld. General Magheru for in his mind he knew he had to get back to Romana and took the next road to the right following traffic to a parallel main route the Victoriei Calea, but it was a one way system and there was no turn right and instead of turning left he drove straight on into a narrow dead end road, which was blocked with cars. As a consequence he had a devil of a job reversing out into the main stream of traffic flow, but as always he succeeded with blaring of horns. I had a new route planned out to carry on down Victoriei Calea, but Roger as always wanted to turn left up some side road, fortunately I persuaded him to carry on down to Regina Elisabeta and turn left to Piaţa Universităţii then take a left again to go up Nicolae Bălcescu keeping insisting he kept to the inside lane as

176

we approached Romana, so we could go around it.

Reaching Piața Romana we circulated around to our turn off, Str. Căderea Bastiliei, where Hotel Unique was situated. The narrow street was one-way only but had a line of stationary traffic. The traffic moved infrequently and for only a few metres at a time so I got out of the car and walked up the road to find the hotel and check out the parking there. About 150m up the road on the left I spotted the glass fronted hotel with a small apron outside used for parking, however a taxi with its doors wide open and no driver was spread across the only two spaces. As I passed its open door to go into the hotel I noticed a wallet and money spread out on the passenger seat. Standing inside the hotel reception were two women but I couldn't communicate with them, as they had no English, or French. However, they indicated that someone would come. In less than a minute the receptionist appeared and spoke very good English to both the taxi driver and the pregnant woman with him. They took a while to settle what ever they were doing and the pregnant woman was given a key after paying some money by credit card. Afterwards she left with the taxi driver to drive off. The receptionist then attended to me. I told him that we wanted to come in and indicated the traffic to him. He replied, "It's September", thinking that it explained it all. He asked me where the car was and I told him but then Linda arrived saying that Roger had parked further back along the road. The traffic outside wasn't moving much so I checked in and was given the key to room 102 and a town map and some information. While Linda waited in one of the hotel's car parking spaces I went down to tell Roger, but he was already driving towards the hotel and was parked within a few minutes.

The rooms looked very good but I had to go down to ask the receptionist how to work the shower in our room. He came up to show me but got a little wet in the process not turning the right knob. It was one of those showers with a great many nozzles and jets with more than one position and angle to actuate water flow.

Two Storey Loggia Hanul lui Manuc

After settling in we all decided to take a walk down into town to relax a little. Bucharest is known for its wide, tree-lined boulevards, glorious Belle Époque buildings and a reputation for the high life, which in the 1900s earned it the nickname of 'Little Paris'. A fanciful

178

Romanian legend has it that a shepherd named Bucur, whose name literarily means 'Joy', founded the city of Bucharest on the banks of the Dambovita River. It is said that his flute playing amazed people and hearty wine offered from nearby vineyards endeared him to local traders.

We had walked down to Romana then further on down passing shops and restaurants to Piața Universității and continued on down Bld. I.C.Bratianu where we found a café-patisserie to sit in the shade at an outside table. I had a cola and a bread roll while the others too had drinks and something to eat. I was pleasantly surprised so far with what I had seen of Bucharest, its buildings were not austere, or the people dowdy, moreover the atmosphere was much like any other major European city. Suitably refreshed we left the café to take a right turn off the boulevard into a network of narrow town streets, some with tables and chairs outside of restaurants and café-bars, until we came at last to an open piazza, near to the river and an entrance to an inn, the Hanul lui Manuc, meaning Manuc's Inn. We entered through a door into a wooden floored bar area and took a passage into an inner courtyard at one storey above the ground. The building was partly undergoing restoration judging from some of the scaffolding.

Hanul lui Manuc is the oldest operating hotel building in Bucharest and within its precincts is a popular restaurant, several bars, a coffeehouse, and facing the street there are several stores as well as an extensive bar. Its massive courtyard is surrounded by a two storey loggia and not only has it hosted many performances and fairs it also has been a popular place for Romanian television crews to shoot costume dramas. The hotel and restaurant were closed down in 2007 for refurbishment but all the shops including a well-known bar, the Cafeaneaua Bucurestilor de Altadata (Bucharest of Yesteryear Cafe), remained open. The hotel and restaurant are expected to reopen under new management once the restoration and refurbishment are complete. Unfortunately there is an on going dispute between the city government and the owners about whether planning permission was given for certain modifications.

The inn has a history and was originally built in 1808. A wealthy Armenian entrepreneur, Emanuel Mârzaian, who is better known under his Turkish name Manuc-bei was its first owner. By the middle of the 19th century it became Bucharest's most important commercial complex with 15 wholesalers, 23 retail stores, 107 rooms for offices, or living quarters, two receiving rooms and a pub. The 'Inn' has had many restorations over the years but has kept its basic structure. It was the site of the preliminary talks for Meetings prior to 'The Treaty of Bucharest', which put an end to the 1806–1812 Russo-Turkish war. At one time theatre performances were held there including the first performance of a Romanian operetta. Important meetings of the Wallachian pro-war party prior to WW1 were held in the 'Sala Dacia' room of the inn. These meetings laid plans to establish a Greater Romania by uniting with Transylvania and Bukovina. Under communist rule the building was nationalized but since the revolution, in 2007, the ownership was restored to Prince Șerban-Constantin Cantacuzino.

We walked around the upper storey of the loggia that surrounded a courtyard café where a man was entertaining the clientele on a keyboard instrument. After taking the stairs down sat at one of the tables and ordered coffee and afterwards gin and tonics for all of us except for Cicely. It was good to sit and listen to the music and gaze around at the old wooden architecture. The place was atmospheric and quite grand and has surprisingly survived the austere years of communist rule and dictatorship.

After buying a ten-journey metro ticket to share we took an underground train from Piaţa Unirii to Piaţa Romana. The metro was clean and pleasant and the train carriages wide and comfortable. The idea of building an underground railway in Bucharest was apparently first mooted in the 1930s and eventually its construction was due to begin in 1941. However, WW2 intervened and it was another four decades before construction could begin. The first part of the metro surprisingly took three years to complete, since the lack of up-to-date tunneling equipment and a mix of sedimentary rock and soft clay made tunneling difficult. The first section to open was Semanatoarea to Timpuri Noi. The metro though wasn't built for traveling around the city centre its original main purpose was for workers to travel from massive housing estates, built during the 1960s and 1970s, to the factories where they worked. Recently the many stations originally named for industrial plants have been renamed attempting to airbrush out the past. Arriving at Piaţa Romana station on Line M2 we found it a bizarre place with platforms hidden behind walls that looked as if it was an afterthought. Of course this is true, in the original plans there was no station at Romana and was only added later at the request of Elena Ceausescu, who had overruled her husband who fully believed the good people of Bucharest did not need a station at Romana for they could easily walk up to Piața Victoriei.

Leaving the metro at Romana went by way of Căderea Bastiliei glancing at two cafés on the way up to the hotel, as a possibility for dinner later. However, our main plan was to look at the Sangria restaurant further up the street that earlier the hotel reception had told us was a good place to eat. Just before getting there a sign in red neon lighting displayed 'Mon Amour'. Thinking this to be a restaurant I went through a yard to check it out. It looked closed but at a door up some steps another notice stated something that was easy to interpret, 'massaging parlour.' I beat a hasty retreat thinking it to be a brothel. Apparently after I walked away Linda and Cicely, who were smiling broadly, said a large lady came out to attend to me. I walked on to the Sangria that was not far up the road and the choice on the menu outside looked good enough to have dinner there later.

I found out about 'Mon Amour' later. Why should one go there an advertisement proclaimed, *'Imagine a place where all dreams can come true, a place where you're always welcome, a place where you can leave your worries behind, a place where you can find the gorgeous girls. Well, that place is Mon Amour Erotic Massage Parlor, it's a place where your wildest fantasies come true in the company of beautiful women. Our girls are chosen not only for their beauty, but also for their commitment to provide quality service to our customers.*

Mon Amour Erotic Massage Parlor is an oasis of bliss and sensuality and provides you an erotic experience that you will never forget.' Perhaps we did miss something but it was not for us.

Later dinner at the Sangria did not turn out to be all that good. Roger had some bad meat, which he offered Linda, as always his taster, she always takes it but this time she didn't realize it was really bad and cursed Roger. The chef agreed it was off when the plate was returned.

It was around seven thirty when we arrived at the Sangria, the evening very warm and pleasant, and entered its doors to a long inn-like open roofless space containing palm trees. Our table was located in an open sided room with stone flooring and archways that looked out onto the entrance courtyard. It was the ground floor of a double-decked loggia. Surrounding our table were a number of potted plants isolating us from other tables where people were already engaged in eating and conversation. I remembered the quote I had seen.

'Many say that Sangria is the most beautiful restaurant in Bucharest. From the outside in the street you have no idea what to expect and you can hear no noise from the clientele. Inside the place is beautifully appointed with both discretion and with taste. It is light and airy with its famous retractable semi-transparent roof. There are plants some very impressive like the large palm trees, stained glass windows and an alley with outdoor lanterns on poles that makes you feel in another world of luxury and amazing interior design. Down the sides

183

under arches there are tables and chairs in stylish leather. The ambiance is quiet and peaceful. Sangria is a beautiful restaurant isolating its guests into an island of music, landscape and good taste with good food and wine. It is a Spanish restaurant that also serves Mediterranean and International food.'

Roger ordered a large carafe of Sangria for us while we perused the large menu. Eventually Roger and I ordered starters. He had a salmon carpaccio and I had the caprese with buffalo mozzarella and green pesto sauce. These were delicious and just right for a warm evening. For the main course I ordered roast rabbit with a wine and berry sauce served with a fresh ratatouille and basmati rice. And when I ate the dish its succulence and taste were divine and when accompanied by a large glass of a heavy dry red wine it was perfection. Both Linda and Cicely had sea bream with a mushroom sauce and mashed potatoes. Roger had a lamb chop sauté potatoes in goose fat and a vegetable salad.

During the meal we talked about various afflictions and medications especially Linda's and also our experiences with Spanish food both good and bad. Partly this was a consequence of Roger's main meal. Throughout he had struggled with a bad chop and that put a bit of damper on proceedings. He always seems to be the one who suffers from his choices of food. Nevertheless, even after experiencing the bad meat and Linda too to some extent, who was asked to sample the meat Roger indulged in a dessert sharing a pancake with Linda. The pancake was served with a ricotta and orange sauce. Neither Cicely nor I had a dessert, I just had an espresso to finish off. Roger also had a latte but wanted a brandy too. And that started us talking about brandies and past experiences we have had. The bar didn't have any French or Italian so I suggested Metaxa, which I like if I am in Greece. Through my persuasion he ordered a Metaxa but when it arrived said it smelt and tasted of drains, so not such a good evening for Roger; but as it turned out he was cultivating a cold and that might have explained the problem. The bill was almost 400 lei for the food and wine even though Roger wasn't charged for his main course, nevertheless we went back to the hotel laughing, it had been an experience.

The air-conditioning failed in the night and we had to open the window and so were woken by traffic noise at 5am. Cicely was disturbed even more throughout the night by a random intermittent ringing noise. The weather forecast on TV indicated that the temperature would be 28 degrees Celsius by mid morning.

We were down at the small breakfast bar by twenty to nine where they had a good buffet selection. The cook who was on duty spoke good English and showed us how to work some of the machines. I had two boiled eggs but the sulphurous vapours from within when I cut into them were too much for Linda's sensitivities, she doesn't like boiled eggs. Fortunately neither her nor Roger suffered any ill effects from the Sangria experience of the night before.

After breakfast, in glorious sunshine, we walked down to Romana from where we took the metro to Piaţa Unirii. On exiting the metro walked across the square to go down Str. Halelor to the junction with Calea Victoriei passing by Hanul Manuc. Walking up Victoriei for a block came across an impressive looking building of the Belle Époque period, which was probably at one time a bank. Opposite a sign pointed along a narrow pavé surfaced lane, Str Stavropoleos, to the Caru' cu Bere restaurant.

Outside the restaurant were some tables and chairs and a reception desk for reservations, which was attended by a couple of young girls dressed in cream skirts, white short blouses and a brownish sleeveless jerkin over the blouse. Frequently they were on the telephone answering calls. Draped from an awning was a sign in green lettering and in English stating, *'probably the best restaurant in town.'* Music emanated from inside as we approached the door to go in.

'Caru' cu Bere is one of the oldest beerhouses in Bucharest, with a good reputation established over many years. It was first opened in 1879, as the Old Zlatari Inn but at the end of the nineteenth century moved to Stavropoleos Street. Each object in the beer house is said to have its own story. It is one of the few places in Bucharest where nothing seems to have changed over the years. Nicolae Mircea, along with his family, played a major role in Caru' cu Bere's story having established it as a both a place to eat and a place to be entertained. Its architecture and décor with murals, carved cross beams and stained glass are reminders of why Bucharest was once considered to be 'Little Paris'. It has an atmosphere reminiscent of its earliest beginnings. A famed icon is *'Old Ghita'*, whose silhouette guards the right crossbeam. Old Ghita was a cellar man who worked there for many years, fetching

186

and carrying by lantern light from a well stocked cellar allegedly crammed full of wine and beer barrels. For many years the house specialty was hot dogs with horseradish sauce and hundreds were consumed every day. Frankfurters, beef salad, black radish and olives were offered for free along with a bottle of wine adding to the general merriment. But nowadays Caru' cu Bere is striving to revive its past tradition by promoting 'real beer' culture. Upstairs, in the beerhouse, you can drink beer brewed using the original family recipe for house-beer, along with food specialties, as a reminder of times past, but for those who want fine dining the old wine cellar is the place to eat and drink, as well as be entertained.

Inside the Belle Époque architecture mixed along with Art Nouveau style didn't disappoint. We sat at one of the tables looking at the blackened paintings probably caused by years of tobacco smoke. I ordered a hot chocolate while Linda ordered a cappuccino, Cicely a tea and Roger a beer. When Cicely's tea arrived she had to ask for some milk, (English fashion) for it is conventionally served black with lemon. According to the menu live music was played during lunch and dinner. We agreed that we would like to have dinner and I went out to make a reservation only to discover that it was full for Tuesday evening except for the basement, so I booked a table in the no smoking area at 19:30 for our last night.

We left the restaurant and turned left along the street to visit the Stavropoleos Monastery Church. It is a bijou church surrounded by modern buildings dating probably from the 1960's and 70's; the area looked a little run down.

Close to the central area, Stavropoleos Monastery is the oldest building in the capital. It was founded in 1724 by a Greek monk, Ioanichie, and built in Byzantine style. The place of worship is representative of late Brâncovenese style and at the back is a small courtyard built in 1899 where there are many columns and graves. The monastery is richly decorated, especially the porch. In the church are some old religious objects recovered from demolished churches during the Communist regime. Life at the monastery is divided between prayer, work and study. Work consists of restoration of old books, icons, liturgical vestments and embroidery, writing and publishing books. Four nuns, a priest confessor and three sisters live in the monastery, which is protected by the Holy Archangels Michael and Gabriel, by St. Justin the Martyr and Philosopher, by St. Bishop Athanasius and by St. Haralambie the Martyr.

We found the Romanian art of the eighteenth and nineteenth century attractive especially the murals and paintings. The church's elegance had been preserved thankfully through the communist period. Of great fun for me were the three smiling angels in a damaged mural on a wall in the courtyard.

After leaving the church headed for the Dâmbovița River and crossed it by a bridge to the edge of Piața Națiunile Unite. The river isn't wide or particularly attractive and has its source in the Făgăraș Mountains and was one time the main source of water for the citizens of Bucharest. We walked along the river for a while before cutting through a network of streets with apartment blocks to emerge at a wide boulevard, Bld. Unirii, which was built to rival the Champs Elysee in Paris. Crossing to the central reservation gardens, where many fountains were strung out along it, we saw in the distance facing us at the far end the monstrous architecture of the Palace of Parliament. To me it looked like a grey-white rectilinear wedding cake dominating its surroundings, not surprising since it was built during the 'Golden Age' of the communist dictatorial regime and born out of the mind of a man for whom the notion of reasonable size did not exist.

How did this come about?

It was the evening of March 4, 1977 when Bucharest experienced a large earthquake measuring 7.3 on the Richter scale. The epicenter was in Vrancea and was felt across the whole Balkan Peninsula In the city it lasted for a minute, during which time almost every building shook wildly and more than 1,500 people died. It was devastating, 35,000 buildings damaged including 33 major ones and many apartment blocks. This gave the dictator, Nicolae Ceausescu, some space to rebuild his capital with his vision of what a socialist city should look like. But he needed more space and the earthquake was used as an excuse to demolish even further buildings that he didn't like. In addition to a Civic Centre he wanted to construct a large palace for himself and his wife, which was to be built on a hill cleared to satisfy his megalomaniac ambitions. The clearances demolished much of Bucharest's historic centre including 19 Orthodox Christian churches, 6 Jewish synagogues, 3 Protestant churches and 30,000 residences.

Walking clockwise around the palace hoping to find the public entrance a security guard at the 'Senate' entrance advised us to go back in an anticlockwise direction to find the public entrance at 'Gate 2'. It seemed like a long walk in the heat of the day but eventually we were through the gate and walking up to the entrance. Inside were some racks of tourist gifts and a main reception desk and area. I went up to get entry tickets but they wanted some id. I had carried Cicely's passport and mine in my zipped shirt pocket, but Roger had theirs locked in the hotel safe. Fortunately Linda had her driving license with her hoping this would do. At first they wouldn't accept it for it had no photograph, but the receptionist got advice from senior security staff and she was able to go in. So it left only Roger who couldn't enter and said he would catch up with us later.

I paid 75 lei for the three of us, as well as extra 30 lei for Cicely to take photographs, and waited for the English Tour to begin. Quite a number of people were waiting, some were Americans and some wore headscarves, obviously Muslims. Ten minutes later we were ushered through the security gates and told to wait again on the steps beyond. Our tour guide was a young woman in her twenties and I discovered later had only been in the job for two months. She spoke good English and hadn't lived under the Communist rule, so had no hang-ups.

Once she gathered us together in the first room she told us that the designer of the building was a 29-year-old woman who had won this accolade through designs submitted in an open competition set by Ceausescu.

190

It was in 1978 after a state visit to Pyongyang in North Korea that the preliminaries for the 'People's House' project began. It started with a design contest that lasted for almost 4 years before the young Anca Petrescu was appointed to the post of chief architect. Mira Anca Victoria Mărculeț Petrescu was Ceausescu's favorite architect and only he and Anka were allowed to know what the eventual structure would look like, resulting in fundamental design failings and a kitsch look. The building's dimensions are huge being 270m by 240m, 86m high and 92m below ground. In all it has 12 levels, and is said to be the second largest building in the world next to the Pentagon building in the United States. Construction began in 1983 involving 700 additional Romanian architects and designers. The building contains 1,100 rooms and all the materials in construction were home produced, including Transylvanian marble, steel, bronze and wood. In addition special crystal chandeliers were manufactured, together with lights and mirrors and of the 200,000 square metres of carpets many were spun and woven on site. No official records exist of the cost and labour used but it is claimed that 20,000 workers were employed on a 24/7 basis. As a result a very large foreign debt was incurred to finance the project and in order to repay the debt Ceausescu triggered a standard of living collapse to an all time low. Food was rationed, and electricity blackouts and gas shortages became an everyday occurrence, as a result the majority of people were deprived, whereas the ruling class exhibited outrageous extravagance. This situation was a melting pot for eventual discontent and angry protest. Ultimately in 1989, as the People's Palace was nearing completion, a reactionary revolution broke out. Mass protests started in Timisoara causing martial law to be declared, a Bucharest rally turned to riot and the Ceausescu's were forced to flee the capital by helicopter but were fortunately captured by police in Targoviste. An ad hoc military court sentenced them to death after finding them guilty of charges ranging from illegal gathering of wealth to genocide. They were executed by firing squad on Christmas Day 1989. In the aftermath the new government moved its functions into the infamous building that was renamed the Palace of Parliament. Today it also houses the National Museum of Contemporary Art, however most of the large uneconomical premises are still unoccupied for they are lacking in proper facilities even for conferences proving the building to be somewhat of a white elephant.

Our guide told us that the 'People's House' project cost 3.3 Billion Euros by the time it was completed but that work was still ongoing especially aimed at reducing the energy needs of the building, as well as increasing its ventilation in more economic ways. The first room we visited was called 'The Theatre'. It was a small theatre with stalls and boxes but the architect had made a fundamental error – there was no back stage, or theatre facilities and what is more the stage was not very deep. I thought this was probably due to her alleged compassion of designing with Lego bricks. Our guide said that they currently use it for conference facilities. One glorious feature is a rock crystal chandelier. It is large, impressive and truly magnificent.

We visited a number of other opulent marble rooms of

considerable size. However they were oppressive with lack of ventilation. Apparently Ceausescu didn't like air-conditioning, as it made him feel cold, and as a consequence ventilation is supplied by small holes located in the ceiling. We only saw 5% of the rooms in the building, but in almost every room we visited our guide said they were used for conferences, yet in only one did we see any facilities.

In a long room you could have run 100m races in and if you left the doors open to the other rooms much more. This massive room was lit from a glass paned ceiling and had on each end wall massive areas to frame large paintings. Supposedly these were originally for portraits of Nicolae and Elena Ceausescu, but Nicolae is said to have changed his mind and narcissistically wanted a mirror opposite his portrait showing him disappearing into infinity; he was executed before this came about. Our guide said that the ballroom had only been used once and that was for the wedding event of Nadia Comăneci, the Olympic gymnastic champion and a Romanian National idol. Apparently she and her American husband were married in an elaborate ceremony there. It became Bucharest's version of a Royal Wedding. Nadia had defected to the USA, where she had met her husband to be, Bart Conner, who was also a gymnast. I well remembered her achievements in the Olympics Games. A slight loveable but earnest girl, I know that her story is very complicated but it is worth a little digression here.

Comăneci was born in Gheorghe Gheorghiu-Dej, now Oneşti, on November 12th, 1961 and when she was married at the age of forty became in 2001 a naturalized citizen of the United States, but she still retained her Romanian passport and dual nationality. At the age of 14 she became a world star. In the 1976 Montreal Olympics she won five medals, three gold, one silver, and one bronze. She also scored a perfect 10 in two events, a score no one previously had achieved. In the 1980 Olympics, she won two gold and two silver medals. The degree of difficulty of her performances together with level of her technical execution resulted in higher future expectations for women's gymnastics and a redefinition of the sport. She defected to the United States in 1989 and in 1996 married the American Bart Conner, a 1984 Olympic gold medalist. Later she and Conner became pioneers in pairs-gymnastics before Comaneci retired from the sport to work both as a coach and a judge. Amongst her other achievements she was the '1976 BBC Sports Personality of the Year', in the overseas athletes category, the Associated Press's 1976 'Female Athlete of the Year', and also the 'UPI Female Athlete of the Year'. Back home in Romania, Comăneci's success led her to be named a 'Hero of Socialist Labour' being the youngest ever in Romania to receive such recognition during the administration of Nicolae Ceauşescu.

At last we entered a room with an open window and breathed a sigh of relief for fresh air was flowing in. The room led out to a large balcony that looked down the Bulevardul Unirii. Apparently a myth has been created concerning Michael Jackson. He was supposed to have addressed the people of Bucharest on his 1992 tour declaring to an enormous crowd of fans from the balcony, "I LOVE BUDAPEST!" He was forced, it is said, moments later to escape by private helicopter. Our guide said that the only truth to the story is that Michael Jackson did say the words but his gaffe was from the National Stadium in Bucharest.

We finished the tour and collected our passports and driving license and just as we had ordered some coffee and cake from a counter in the foyer Roger turned up and joined us. He said he had been into the National Costumes Exhibition next door and also looked at a demonstration that was taking place in the Parcul Izvor across the way towards the river.

I left Roger in the foyer to walk over to the park while the girls went around the exhibition that Roger had visited. A few people were still there with placards but most of the demonstrators were packing stuff away in boots of cars. They were animal rights people and were protesting about some new legislation that was going through parliament about what action to take for stray dogs in Bucharest. The park was an open space with a children's play area in a far corner and a few public statues, not much else to see so I walked back to the palace. The others were just leaving the foyer when I met them. The girls said that they had been impressed with the traditional costumes on display. They were from different parts of Romania or used in different festivals. The style of the fabrics and the intricacies of the sewing all added to their fascination with the displays.

We walked across the park noticing layers of white feathers on the ground looking as if it had been raining them. They were all over the place. Roger said he had been told that there had been a festival of pillow fights, but when I got home discovered that there was a little more to it than that.

There had been a performance by a French theatre company, 'Les Studios de Cirque', early the previous day. The performance marked the 'Day of Bucharest' that celebrates the day when the Romanian capital was first mentioned in public records. King, Vlad Tepes, signed the actual document on Sept. 20, 1459. This brutal king, who punished criminals by impaling, is said to have inspired Bram Stoker's fictional character Dracula. However, today white feathers are used to celebrate the city of Bucharest where families take part in their scattering.

Heading back took a riverside path to a bridge to cross the river to Calea Victoriei and walked up to the old covered arcades of the Pasajul Villacrosse. This survivor arcade of a previous era, built in 1891, is covered with glass and constructed in an elongated horseshoe shape and is named after the architect, Xavier Villacrosse. We stopped at a café-bar in an bright open space at the loop in the passage where there were other cafés too. Sitting at one of the tables we ordered ice creams but they turned out to be nondescript and probably made from powder. After this short break left the arcade from the loop end to Str. E Carada and turned right into Str. Doamnei. On reaching Str Ion Ghica turned left up it heading towards Piaţa Universităţii where near to the top end of the road an attractive colourful Russian orthodox church drew our attention. The church named St Nicholas Students' Church was built in 1905 using donations from Tsar

Alexander II. The building is topped with seven, typically Russian, onion domes and crowned with an Orthodox cross. The wooden, gold-gilded iconostasis is allegedly a copy of the altar in Arhangelsk Cathedral, in Moscow's Kremlin. Inside the dim light made it difficult to see the numerous images many of which were of beautiful female saints. It was a well worthwhile visit.

In Piața Universității we took the metro to Piața Romana and from there walked back to the hotel. There we asked the receptionist to book a table for us at the hotel's Lebanese restaurant, Unique Bistro, located in the restaurant district of the old town. Roger said we would go by taxi, as it would only cost 10 lei according to the receptionist, so we didn't need any detailed instructions for how to get there. We made arrangements to meet beforehand in our room for an aperitif at seven, after arranging dinner for 19:45 hours and a taxi pick up at seven thirty.

After a rest and a shower and a change of clothes we met up for our soiree as agreed before going down to the lobby to await the taxi. The taxi was a little late and took us on what seemed like a long drive to drop us off near to the Munuc Inn and said that was it. We got out a little confused but Roger phoned the hotel desk that informed him that the bistro was on a corner nearby. This was too vague for the restaurant was nowhere to be seen from the little square where we stood. Near to were many restaurants, all crowded with people. I went into one of the restaurants and asked for directions but neither of the waitresses I talked to knew of the place. When I came out into the square once more I found that Roger had had more success, he had made friends with

197

a bunch of taxi drivers and got them using mobile phones to discover the whereabouts of our bistro from the hotel receptionist. At last we got the right instructions and found it not on a corner but up a busy street Str. Franceza.

We were guided to a table on the outside terrace for the evening was still very warm. The menu was large with many attractive dishes. Roger ordered a mixed grill for his main course and thinking this to be for one I ordered three small plates and a salad. We both ordered the Lebanese bread that is similar to the flat bread that we had had in Istanbul, the one that blows up like a balloon. My plates were, chicken livers in a pomegranate sauce, four ostrich sausages and four deep-fried coated minced lamb balls with grilled mushrooms. The girls were more sensible in their choices but there details I have forgotten. Before our courses arrived the waiter tried to sell us some special wine, he must have thought us an easy touch. He brought to our table six assorted bottles of wine that were not on the menu, but at 700 lei each. We gave an emphatic no saying that the menu wines were only 45 lei. He seemed a little flustered and tried to explain about the price being in old currency but it was probably a scam. We ordered a Cabinet Sauvignon at 45 lei that was very good to have with the meal.

Roger's plate when it arrived was so enormous, it was meant for two people. It had almost everything you could think of in great quantities. He wanted us to help him out but we also had more than enough to contend with, although Linda ever the martyr did have some. Roger struggled through but probably didn't consume half of it. The wine ran out and Roger ordered a large glass of the same to finish. I ordered an espresso. Throughout the meal the conversation flowed with many jokes making it an hilarious evening and great fun.

We walked to a metro nearby. It was part of the Piaţa Unirii complex but we had to walk a long way underground before we reached our line to take us to Piaţa Romana.

The next day was cloudy with little sunshine. We were all down for breakfast at quarter to nine and found Roger not feeling too good, he had almost lost his voice and whatever was affecting him had worsened considerably. I tried the blue cheese and some of the feta-like cheese with bread from a selection of the boutique rolls that were in the buffet. One of the rolls was reddish probably indicating capsicum within the recipe.

We agreed to visit the National Museum in the morning to view the art displays and set out on our journey about ten. When we reached Piaţa Romana I exchanged some money to make sure that I had enough lei to pay the hotel and restaurant bills. Then from Romana we walked Str. Mendeleev and continued on down Str. Clemenceau to Piaţa Enescu by the Athénée Palace Hilton hotel that was built in 1914 and also the Ateneul Romãn (Romanian Athenaeum).

It was in 1865 that leaders in the Romanian cultural and scientific field founded the Romanian Atheneum Cultural Society and a French architect, Albert Galleron, designed a building that served the society. It was inaugurated in 1888, although work continued until 1897. A portion of the construction funds was raised by public subscription but took twenty-eight years. A slogan used at the time is still remembered today: *'Donate one leu for the Ateneu!'*. An important event was held in the building in December 1919. It was an international conference that led to the unification of Bessarabia, Transylvania and Bukovina with the Old Kingdom of Romania and to constitute a new Greater Romania. In recent times since the collapse of the communist state extensive reconstruction and restoration work has taken place to save the building from collapse. The building is now the City's main concert hall and home to the George Enescu Philharmonic Orchestra and an annual international music festival.

We gazed at the neoclassical building for some time, looking through a fence to the gardens and the building beyond on which important figures were depicted in a frieze before walking down to the linked square, Piața Revoluției, where a large statue of Carol 1 on horseback stood outside the university library facing the former royal palace. The statue had recently been erected by the City council to replace a statue that had been removed and destroyed by the communists in the 1940's.

The Palace was built around 1815 by Prince Dinicu Golescu but through the years has had many alterations. The French architect Paul Gottereau, remodeled it in the 1880's only for it to be rebuilt again 1930-1938 after being severely damaged by a fire in

1926. In 1948 the palace was used to house the National Art Collection, displaying an extensive collection of both Romanian and European art dating from the 15th to the 20th century, but the building was damaged again during the revolutionary events of December 1989 and was subsequently closed for several years to undergo repairs.

After crossing the square to the former old palace we found the entrance gates locked to what is now the National Gallery of Art. A young woman, standing nearby, told us that the gates didn't open until 11 o'clock that was in another ten minutes. To save waiting in the open, as Roger was croaking badly, took a walk around a corner to an eighteenth century Orthodox church.

It's a beautiful red brick church and is one of the oldest churches in Bucharest. Commissioned in 1722 by the boyar Iordache Cretulescu and his wife Safta, a daughter of Prince Constantin Brancoveanu, the church was built in a style created by Constantin Brâncoveanu, a seventeenth century ruler of Wallachia, who set out to create a distinctive national genre of architecture seen earlier at another church. The Brâncovenese Style blends Byzantine and Western architectural elements together with indigenous forms. Although the church suffered damage during the 1989 revolution it has been recently restored. The frescoes in the porch are especially beautiful. Inside there are fragments of late nineteen-century frescoes created by the Romanian artist, Gheorghe Tattarescu. To the side of the church stands a memorial bust of Corneliu Coposu who spent 17 years in prison for his anti-communist activities and was awarded the Legion d'Honeur by the French Government.

Inside the walls, ceiling and inner parts of the dome were covered with iconic frescoes with some of the images I hadn't seen before. The brief time we had gazing upon the art was a pleasing encounter before leaving for the National Gallery of Art. Bought tickets for both the Romanian and European galleries, which were in different wings of the building. Romania Art was on the first floor where we found a comprehensive selection of medieval works that featured some salvaged from many national monasteries but chiefly those from Transylvania and Moldavia. According to the pamphlet we were given, there were 9,500 pieces exhibited in seven rooms. Some of these rooms held objects in precious metals, jewelry and for costume accessories. The first room we entered had icons, a triptych, some carved oak doors from a church and some carved stone objects. I drifted around the rooms looking at the paintings on display, which were interesting to me mainly by their content.

For instance there was a large figurative painting of what I took to be St George fighting a dragon. In the picture sitting behind St. George on the white horse was a small boy wearing a turban and carrying a spouted vessel, this was something that I hadn't seen before in any images of St. George. In another painting, which was of the Last Supper, Jesus was with the twelve apostles, which I counted. Judas was easily identified holding a bag giving the impression of unseen gold, but before Jesus was a head of a curly haired blond boy on a plate. This image was most strange and I couldn't think what it might represent. In yet another painting of the Holy Trinity, there were three identical young men. Behind the man on the right was an image of the Madonna and behind the one on the left an image of an old man. Did this represent the ages of man or from the left God the Father, the Holy Ghost and Jesus? Other strange paintings were of 'The Dormition of Mary'. There were three or four different ones of these on display but the images were more or less the same. Mary lay prostrate with Jesus sitting above her holding a baby in his arms probably representing Mary.

I have since discovered that, 'The Dormition of the Virgin Mary' is her falling asleep at the end of her time on earth. It is not simply called the 'Death of the Virgin' because of a tradition that soon after her soul left her body the two were reunited and taken up to Heaven in what is called the 'Assumption.' A variety of accounts of the Dormition were written in Greek and other eastern languages during the fourth and fifth centuries, some of them with possible roots in the second century. By the sixth century though Latin texts deal with the subject, and by the time of the 13th-century's 'Golden Legend' a large number of versions of the story were in circulation and often inconsistent with each other in matters of detail. This variety explains the diversity of artistic treatments of the subject. Surviving Byzantine icons of the Dormition of the Virgin Mary go back to the ninth century and in a tenth century example the basic image for both East and West is formed.

Up on the second floor were more modern paintings, mostly from 1830 to the current day. Amongst them were some particularly good portraits. One of them I recall was of a peasant girl with a pout who was painted full face and was displayed in an oval frame set in a rectangular gilt frame. Another was of a white-faced girl with red lips surrounded by dark paint. Yet another outstanding one was of a gypsy girl and lastly a portrait of an old Jewish man carrying a goose.

There were still at lot of things to see but we needed a break and a drink too so left the gallery to join Roger, who had left some time before. Roger not looking too well was sitting under a bronze statue of a nude woman. A cold wind blew, so decided to forget about the European Gallery and find a restaurant for lunch. After crossing the square cut through lanes to Bulevardul Nicholae Bălcescu just north of Piața Universității where we found a restaurant with a warm interior. Three of us ordered soup but Roger, as ever a glutton for punishment, ordered sausage, bacon and beans. We all had an Ursus beer to drink and sat back discussing what we had seen in the morning.

After lunch Roger decided to leave us and go back to the hotel to rest while Cicely, Linda and I walked down towards Piața Unirii where, according to our Lonely Planet Guide, we would find the Unirea Department Store, said to be a good place to shop. But before we got to the store the girls were attracted to a clothing shop and went in. Following them I set off the security alarm at the entrance that affected my pacemaker giving me a higher heart rate and a funny feeling down my left arm. The people in the shop didn't appear to be too concerned but I showed them my card and someone understood and switched off the alarm to let us leave.

The department store was no longer as indicated in our Guide but was a Shopping Centre built on 5 floors with many franchises. I said I would meet up with the girls later in the café area on the top floor where I would be sitting in the corner of the chocolatier café. While the girls browsed the shops, I drifted through the floors exploring what there was including a bookshop where I spent some time, getting my heart and arm back to normal.

Later I found a table in the café where a young woman served me. She spoke good English and advised me to have a chocolate cake and a chocolate drink, so I took her advice and ordered them. A little while later she brought the cake and drink over saying not to drink the chocolate until it had cooled down. She saw me looking at a map of Bucharest and said could she help me and came in close pointing out a few places of interest. I found that she had learnt to speak English at school but didn't get enough practice, as she liked to speak it.

The funny feeling down my arm had worn off by the time Cicely and Linda arrived, but I hadn't finished my drink or cake and Cicely was disgusted, especially with the drink. When the waitress laughed Cicely shouted cholesterol, but I don't suffer from a high level unlike her. Linda sat down and ordered an iced coffee with ice cream and cream, while Cicely ordered a tea. Cicely mumbled on about the excess chocolate I had had,

We took the metro back to Piaţa Romana and walked back to the hotel.

Later I went down to the lobby to use the Web to

reserve our flight seats and printed off the boarding cards for the next day. The main difficulty I had was with the printer for it was both a cheap machine and used very thin paper. Nevertheless with a little help from the receptionist I managed to print off all the boarding cards.

At ten to seven we telephoned from reception for a taxi to take us to the bottom end of Str. Stavropoleos, that would be only be a short walk in to the Caru' cu Bere restaurant. It came quite quickly and we were soon being dropped off costing us 7 lei, but we gave the driver 10 lei.

The restaurant was filling up fast as we took our table in the no smoking area. As soon as the waiter came over we ordered two bottles of a Moldavian Cabernet Sauvignon and some water and also a small beer for Roger. The place was so noisy that I could hardly hear what the others were talking about. I ordered a starter of smoked salmon and gravlax with a piping of cheese and dill. For the main course I ordered pork shank off the bone served with a ragout of beans, potatoes and bacon. The evening progressed with food wine and entertainment.

Entertainment started with traditional dancers, Dansuri Populare; then progressed through traditional music, Muzka Populara; to ballroom dancing, Dansuri de Societate and ended with Spanish dancing, 'Dansuri Spaniole'. It was all too noisy for me, couldn't hear the music properly, nor see the dancing. The others got up from the table to go where they could see and took some video and photographs. At the ending of the last two dance sessions professional dance couples came around to the tables asking people if they would like to dance. Linda got up twice to do this and enjoyed it very much, especially the Spanish where she looped around waving her scarf, Roger and I declined politely every time.

For dessert I had an espresso and a slice of cheesecake, Cicely a creamy brownie, Linda pears in red wine. Roger too seemed much better and enjoyed his food. The service we had was excellent but the place was so raucous I had difficulty with conversation and to see the dances, I could only speculate at times for the activities were mostly blocked by pillars or people.

After paying the bill we walked back to the end of the road, I glad to be out in the peace and quiet. A number of taxis were parked ready for clients and I encouraged the others into a taxi that looked the same as the ones we had used before but unfortunately didn't look close enough and the end result was fiasco.

Bucharest's taxi drivers view anyone as fair game when it comes to ripping people off. Locals, foreigners, young, and old, male, female literally anyone who steps in the wrong kind of taxi can expect to be well and truly shafted. The important thing is to spot trusted taxi company operators, which are usually fine, from independents, which are usually bad. But how to spot the difference is the key. By and large, trustworthy taxis are easy to spot as they are emblazoned with the name and phone number of the company they are associated with. To counter this, however, the independents have also started to plaster phone numbers over their cars alongside copycat logos that look cunningly like those of decent taxi companies. The best way to avoid being ripped off is to pay careful attention to the tariffs, displayed on the driver and passenger door of all taxis. There should be one single tariff displayed, and anything higher than 1.69 lei per kilometre should start ringing alarm bells. You have to be extra careful around Piata Universitatii, Piata Unirii and in the Old Town

But I hadn't taken enough care being at that time ignorant of the practices. Shortly after the taxi drove off the driver told us it was after 10 o'clock so that the charge would be double and when we arrived outside of our hotel he charged us 90 lei. This was outrageous and although Roger argued with him he still paid 50 lei so we were well and truly ripped off. The man in the reception was sympathetic and did try to help for a time but I hadn't looked closely enough at the taxi before entering it. It had displayed on it three times the normal price, so in the end we paid almost double this; it left a bad taste, as we left for our beds.

It was the day of the flight back to Heathrow in the afternoon. I had a bit of a hangover from dinner the previous evening and wondered how the others were feeling. The day was bright and sunny, so was some compensation. I remembered Roger saying that we should visit the National Village Museum in the morning so I looked up a route to take.

Took breakfast as usual at nine and checked out around ten thirty paying our bill with Euros before driving off. The first part of the route was easy to Piața Victoriei and then to Piața Charles de Gaulle. The museum was situated just beyond Arcul de Triumf in the Herăstrău Park. However we didn't make the left turn we should have taken at Piața Charles de Gaulle and carried straight on into a dense stream of traffic. Following a railway line on the wrong side of the park we passed by an official City Council party in the middle of the road inspecting a new tramway; TV cameras accompanied them. There are, as in many cities, a great number of one-way streets but after stopping at a road into the park I got my bearings and indicated to Roger the route to follow, but Roger who wanted to go back to Piața Charles de Gaulle. Nevertheless I persuaded him to take my route following the park around to Piața Presei Libere and turn off there, making sure we were in the right lane to turn into the museum entrance. Thus by going down Bulevardul Mărăști to Arcul de Triumf to get into the feeder lane for the Museum entrance. Roger did this well never questioning my instructions even though at one point he wanted to cut through to the park, which would have meant going around the loop again.

Roger parked the car in the shade of some trees and we went over to the entrance and ticket office. It indicated pensioners 3 lei but the woman on the desk made us pay the full adult amount of 6 lei per person, as we were not Romanians. I think this was against EU directives but the amount is so low it was pointless to argue.

The Village Museum was opened in 1936 and contains over 300 wooden houses, windmills, watermills, and churches from all over the country. Many of the buildings are saved originals, which were brought in pieces and reassembled in the park, the oldest houses dating from the seventeenth century. The idea for the Village museum came about through the ethnographer Dimitrie Gusti who wanted the museum to mirror as closely as possible aspects of rural life in past times. The open museum is set out to imitate a real village with clusters of houses and other buildings that are linked by winding paths, some of which at times go alongside of the lake in the park. The buildings are grouped by region, such as Transylvania, Moldova, Dobrogea and so on. Between 1925 and 1935, Gusti assembled a team of specialists to explore the countryside and document village life. Their excellent fieldwork produced invaluable research material including a wealth of photographs, which are in the process of being digitized. The same teams of specialists also acquired during their investigations many artifacts. These were used, or displayed, to add reality to rural life as it was.

A beautiful sunny day added to the experience as we drifted in a peaceful time warp through trees and buildings. There were examples of water driven mills for many village crafts and trade purposes from mining to clothing, each had good explanatory labels and well-assembled tools and machinery that we tried to fathom out how it all worked. Windmills with wooden sails and post steerage were fascinating too for they must have lost most of their energy gained through inertia and friction when in use. The structure of a wooden church looked like it was assembled from an Ikea flat pack for its massive wooden beams interlocked perfectly and faded painted images on the outside walls added to its charm. The various buildings with their furnishings and interior design reflected different parts of the country from which they came. Different construction methods too were clearly demonstrated from wooden cabins to underground rooms topped with reed thatch. The low

Old Water Mill in Village Museum

thatched buildings, from the Danube Delta were basically camouflaged to fit in with their surroundings, as a protection to invasion. At one point we took a break to have a drink in a building used as a café and afterwards Roger still not feeling too good, went back to the entrance to wait for us. The girls and I then slowly strolled back alongside of the lake passing by boat sheds with old fishing boats from the Delta to eventually return to Roger, who was sitting in the shade of a tree. Together once more we looked around the museum shop before leaving for the airport. They had a large range of traditional craftwork but the prices

211

were much higher than we would have paid in the villages.

It was 2 o'clock when we drove off going by way of Piața Presei Libere to continue on to Route 1. The sun was on our back as we continued our journey crossing over the ring road to Otopeni and the airport. The car hire guy was waiting for us as we pulled in to Departures but after unloading the baggage Roger had to go to the desk to collect the 300 lei deposit. We didn't wait long and were soon moving through security checks unfortunately for me I had forgotten about a medical case with scissors and tweezers that was in my backpack, as it increased the hassle for I had to remove my belt and boots as well as emptying my backpack for security staff to discover any other offending metal objects. But they eventually accepted everything.

The sky was still clear as we took off 15 minutes late and enjoyed the in-flight meal before landing on time at Heathrow after an uneventful smooth flight. We were fast through passport control and baggage claim and only had to wait a short time for the bus to take us to the car park where we arrived just after seven. Roger feeling much better drove us back home. A few days later Linda had caught Roger's cold.

Bucharest had been interesting but I enjoyed the other places we had been to and the people we had seen and talked to. Romania is a very pleasant and rewarding country and has much to offer any visitor.